Born Again To Rebirth

Gabriel D. Roberts

I dedicate this book to my friend, Bobby

May you rest in peace, my vagabond friend.

INTRODUCTION

It is from a perspective of great sincerity and heartfelt conviction that I write this book. Many years have passed since I first began to question my Christian faith and I cannot say with any degree of honesty that it has been easy. I have lost friends and even relatives for a time. I have found myself in dismal conditions with people who provided temporary friendship in exchange for the use and abuse of my own. I've seen the dark underbelly of this society and the final destination it takes you to, but I have also seen rebirth and renewal. I have stared at the sunrise with tears in my eyes, inspired by the wonder of this ever-enchanting world in which we live.

Any book on a matter of personal faith will be subject to speculation, debate and conjecture, but I feel it must be shared. I expect many to cast opinion about it without even reading it at all. I cannot help where others are in their personal growth and spiritual endeavors, I can only live my life and do my best to share in the joys and pains of my own path.

This book is for you who are perhaps at a personal crossroads and need a little encouragement, care and understanding. The story of my spiritual journey is a mirroring of the story of countless souls who have crossed the great precipice of the Christian faith into an unknown and frightening world. I strongly believe in the eternal soul and that it is subject to rules of order just as our human bodies are subject to the laws of physics here on earth. However, my time in this life is not over and the jury is not out as to the perfect order in which all things are and will be, that doesn't mean I don't have an educated opinion on what I think is the answer. The ultimate uniting factor in all faiths is the underlying message of love. In matters of faith, love is where we should begin and end, so shall it be with this book. I hope that you will find inspiration from this book and that you will find your happiness in whichever path you choose to travel.

Peace and Love,
Gabriel D. Roberts

FOREWORD

Gabriel and I met in 1999 in the church I was raised in that my father pastored. He was the guitar player in a local band. I remember he played a Gibson Flying V and always had the same sunglasses on, day or night. He was a leader and a inspiring figure in the religious world we both grew up in.

I walked away from the church, religion, and Christianity around the age of 17. When Gabe and I finally reconnected, we were both at a very similar cross roads in our lives; one that involved a lot of whiskey and a lot of drugs. There was something special about experiencing that time with him. I remember feeling like we had something to prove, that we had to show all those authority figures that told us what we could and couldn't do our whole lives just how much we didn't care. It was punk rock, it was dangerous, it was perfect.

For 6 months I slept on Gabriel and his wife Elizabeth's couch in Brooklyn, New York. My addiction to Heroin had take over and I had lost control. Out of all the people I was raised with growing up in church; the place where love and compassion was preached, Gabriel was the one that stood by my side; that loved me whether I was right or wrong, that never once gave up on me.

His journey has been amazing to watch. His wisdom and integrity is inspiring and genuine. He's my brother, my best friend and my hero.

-Robert Patrick

FOREWORD

Religion is for people who're afraid of going to hell. Spirituality is for those who've already been there." — Vine Deloria

I met Gabriel Roberts about two years ago through his wife Elizabeth Raab who was dating a mutual friend at the time. I had been frequenting some of the same music venues and pubs in Seattle in 2005 and I hung out in some of the same circle of musicians, artists, and aspiring writers that Elizabeth would be accustomed to showing up at. There was always a gathering of people at this one bar across the street from the Space Needle that were fun, easy going and would carry themselves with a devil may care attitude especially within the rockabilly and punk rock community. Conversation for the most part was effortless with a feeling of mutual acceptance. It was its own tight knit community

7

and I had never encountered anything like it before. Not even in the church, It wouldn't be until sometime after Gabriel and Elizabeth married before relocating to NYC in 2009 that my wife and I would become good friends with both her and Gabriel through social networking sites. What I didn't know was that the man that I had so innocuously added to our social network of friends would have such a lasting impact on my own personal growth as a former fundamentalist Christian and help me come to terms with some of my own personal demons growing up within the constructs of an evangelical Christian belief system. To this day this book has given me a whole new perspective and insight in to the idea of the things which we are taught to believe as truth as children without questioning and that which we adopt as truth and that everyone else needs to accept as fact or burn for it.

When Gabriel first approached me to contribute to his forthcoming book by writing the forward, I thought he was either drunk, kidding, or had lost his collective mind. What could I possibly share about two of my darkest moments in life that was a direct result of growing up in the church? And then the tears came. I started remembering even in a more visceral way the collection of pictures and moments of absolute terror growing up in a religious and physically abusive home under the hands of my mother and then I began to cry. After several conversations with Gabriel and struggling in dealing with wanting to face my own past, and fractured understanding of unconditional love and religion as a whole, I took my first step towards healing from years of self-hatred and hurt. Even after a couple of months, of stopping and starting the project, I called him and told him that I was really finding it difficult in figuring out how to open his book and I really wanted to do it justice, telling him that if he didn't want to go with what I had submitted before the book goes to press, I wouldn't be hurt or offended. I know now that what I was really doing was looking for an out so I could avoid having to open the closet door to my childhood and turn on the light because I still believed that the monsters and demons were still waiting for me in there, and they were patient. This irrational fear I had was based in a prayer my mother would have me recite when I would hear strange noises at night or be unable to sleep because of a bad dream.

Ghoulies and ghosties and long legged beasties,

And things that go bump in the night (pause)

Good Lord, deliver us.

Sometimes she would even make an ugly face before reciting the last line. Monsters were real. Because it was only the Lord that could protect us from these things that were in the house, right?

Gabriel simply said in his very soft spoken way "I believe in you". Words I haven't heard from very many people most my life. For the first time since entering therapy for anger management and what I perceived as un-explainable panic attacks in 2009, I realized after reading his story that I was going to have to confront years of psychic and spiritual pain and confusion due to my inability to reconcile all the shame and guilt and fear that drove me to such self-destructive behavior and legal troubles that almost cost me my life more than a few times but most notably in the early morning of December 3rd, 2000. It wasn't so much Gabriel's story of growing up in a fundamentalist belief system of religion that moved me as much as it was how closely his experience with Christian fundamentalism in the church mirrored mine. With one major twist. Although we had both attended bible college, studied scripture, prayed and led people to the Lord, using music through Christian rock bands to minister and convey our message of hope to a lost world and attended mega non-denominational church's, above all we both wanted to save the millions of lost souls from a fiery furnace where people who refused to believe in Jesus would be subjected to eternal torment; or for those who just couldn't accept the simplicity of the Gospel story and accept the free gift of salvation. The one defining difference was the author received his BA degree in theology from Seattle Bible College and I was asked to leave Northwest Bible College June of 1987 due to my repeated violations of their drinking smoking and promiscuity, and chapel/class attendance policies. But most importantly, we both had a crisis of faith during and after we had left college and the church.

We both experienced first -hand how quickly the pendulum can swing to the extreme of either side be It self-righteous indignation and intolerance of other peoples beliefs or cultural perspectives in regard to spirituality, or the proverbial middle finger we wear as a badge of honor and justified rebellion to rise against society only to begin living and breathing in the shadows of night risking are very lives to survive, unable to face the truth about our fragile human existence, and the very real truth that we just didn't have all the answers. And the truth is we never did.

Case in point:

From The Seattle Times: Man pulled from Elliott Bay December 3, 2000

SEATTLE--A man was hospitalized suffering from hypothermia after he was pulled from Elliott Bay yesterday morning, police said.

The 35-year-old Ballard resident was spotted by the crew of the ferry Kitsap about 200 yards from Pier 50 at about 3:37 a.m., said Sean O'Donnell, spokesman for the Seattle Police Department. Crew members of a boat launched from the ferry plucked the man out of the water, O'Donnell said.

The man was taken to Harborview Medical Center, where he was listed yesterday in serious condition, said a nursing supervisor.

The man told police he and a friend had been assaulted and chased by some unknown assailants.

That night I was in full flight from reality. Truth be told, looking back on that early cold winter morning when I took that leap off the pier with a headful of cocaine and whiskey is that it just didn't matter anymore. I wanted to die. I was tired of living in the pain of self-abuse and the blind willingness to become a pawn at the hands and agendas of others in exchange for temporary companionship or the next big thrill. To my best recollection in the hours leading up to that near fateful morning after an evening of drinking and several lines of coke is that the "cocktail effect" took over and all the separate conversations in the room became audible and so did my increasing paranoia of my surroundings. That was the moment when I suddenly got up and bolted out the door down the stairs from the above Belltown street view apartment into the darkness of the morning. The fear of being assaulted, violated and robbed had gripped my heart and my psyche again as soon as I hit the street. I heard a person on the sidewalk say, "there goes another one" most likely referring to just another coked up fool out in the city at 3 am doing God knows what. At this point I started running blindly towards the Alaska Way Viaduct in the rain towards the on ramp, headed south towards Seattle's industrial district.

After several attempts to flag down a couple of vehicles and a truck that almost hit me, I crossed to the left side of the freeway where I saw a roof top about 10 feet down, maybe more, and I jumped, landed on the rooftop. I remember looking down from the roof and how dark it was on one side of the roof and still considerably high 20-30 feet from the ground and the alley below. I walked over to the edge of the building and almost had this feeling of being a superhero on high alert but completely unprepared for what was next. I was Batman without a utility belt.

Then the anger kicked in. Forget the church! Forget parents! Forget authority,! Forget love. To hell with fear, to hell with pain, to hell with it all. It was at this point drenched by the morning rain that I noticed there was this bridge-like structure that appeared to cross between the two tiered viaduct underneath it that led to the waterfront.

I started running again, and I kept running until I reached a Pier down on the waterfront. I was tired of living in the unexplained paranoia, being afraid in the absence of fear, tired of living in depression and anxiety that, almost 10 years later would be diagnosed as PTSD from the trauma I sustained due to the psychological and physical abuse I went through as a child; the attempted exorcisms performed by some of the youth group members of two different churches. I had also been terrorized and blindsided by an incident at a house party in Lake Hills, Bellevue where I was unwittingly drugged; facing the very real threat of being kidnapped and murdered. After years with a history of going to jail, hospitals, court ordered treatment centers, and eventually winding up homeless and back on the street, I just didn't care anymore. I wanted everything to stop.

I ran down toward the pier and just kept running until I reached an opening with a small chain link fence gate and jumped into the water and started swimming away from shore towards the frigid open waters of Elliot Bay. And though it may sound completely insane to anyone who has never dealt with the futile attempts through the use and abuse of alcohol and drugs, to numb the inner torment, to deafen the voices of sins shame the hissing whispers of hell's damnation and the pain of being terrorized with pronouncements of being evil, possessed by demons, while being beaten within an inch of your life only to be told by one of the biggest evangelical churches in Washington state the very same thing a few years later...

All I can say is that even though the air was below freezing and the water was somewhere between 35-44 degrees; I knew if I kept swimming towards the middle of the bay I would no longer be in pain and for the first time in years I saw a glimmer of hope even though I would soon be taking my last breath and pass on to the other side or nothingness. I felt a warmth come over my body that I hadn't felt since my first real kiss with a girl named Connie back in my cousin's tree house in the summer of 78 in my hometown of Maple Valley. What I didn't know was that six years later after surviving this night, I would feel that same warmth again when I experienced true genuine unconditional love. The moment I looked in to the eyes of my future wife Sandra I knew I was home and for the first time in my life, I felt safe.

What happened next I can only describe as a purposeful gradual end to what I knew as my concept of God, Jesus and religion as whole, and a magical initiation into a new beginning of self - discovery. I swam further out from shore into the denser fog that was now coming off the water and I started to tire. Breathing heavily, I began to speak the words "I'm sorry".

The immediate paranoia and fear I was feeling was gone. I was ready. For what I did not know, but I was ready. The next thing I remember was looking ahead of me in the darkness with the smell of sea salt getting stronger and I saw what I thought was a string of lights in the distance illuminating through the fog and reflecting off of the water. It just kept getting brighter and closer to where I was bobbing off shore. I heard someone shout there's someone in the water and I heard a loud horn sound and then silence.

Real life can get messy. That's just the truth of life. There are no half hour sitcom happy endings, or movie happily ever after's in the real world. With genuine love comes the pain of hard work and commitment. And sometimes because of our human fragility and character flaws we fail miserably. But we keep trying. After that night, there wasn't an immediate "Aha" moment of revelation or spiritual awakening that took place. For the next five years I would I still attempt to numb years of pain by almost any means necessary. It wouldn't be until almost a year after my marriage on the very strong suggestion of my wife to seek therapy for my sudden outbursts of anger and panic attacks, that the shell of my heart would be broken wide open and I would begin the process of healing with a woman named Danielle.

She taught me that trust can only come when you feel someone's presence is authentic. She showed me that the only person I had been rebelling against was myself.. She reflected the truth about my being in a state of shock as a child with compassion, gentle direction and love, with my wife beside me every step of the way. Since 2009 I have begun to peel back the layers of my worst childhood memories and nightmares that had haunted me for years and had become a reality that followed me into my adulthood. I would learn over the next four years that not only can trauma have a crippling effect in one's personal life; it can kill the human spirit and the will to survive. It was time for me to take personal responsibility for my own spiritual and mental well-being. It was time to face the fear of hell, demons and the false beliefs about myself head on and without reservation of all that I was taught growing up as child, and that of which I would later be subjected to by well-intentioned Christians who in their own fear of the supernatural and mortality, project on others that which we fear the most. The unknown

Today I still have Christian family and friends who did not just cast me aside when I left the church. I would be remiss not to mention a family that helped me out of a very dark time and I do not want to paint a broad generalized brush that all evangelical Christians are the same when it comes to the hell -fire brimstone persuasion approach. I actually dreamt about this one family the night before writing this and am still in touch with two of the members in our social network from time to time. After spending almost seven plus months in a substance abuse focused program through the Union Gospel mission in the early nineties where one of their daughters was doing an internship, they took me into their home the following Fall and helped me get back into school. Not a bible college but a secular community college. They loved me as one of their own. It felt like a real family. I believe they were genuine and authentic to the core of what they believed. But during that time of my stay with them I started to question their motives for helping me, and now looking back I know why. It was hard to believe I was deserving of love because I didn't love myself. I hid behind a false bravado and made sure I was heard, when the truth of the matter was I was terrified of my own shadow.

What I know now is this. It's the paths we take and the choices we make in our journeys that makes being a participant in life such a miracle. And when one is fortunate enough to stumble in to the arms of someone who cares for you and loves you for who you are and not because you have It all figured out, and isn't afraid to tell you the truth about yourself at the risk of hurting one's ego and teaches you to love yourself the good, the bad, and the ugly? It was time to wake up. Though, I had spent my whole life running from love, when I finally let my guard down and opened up my heart I began to experience the vulnerability and trust of a child again. Love had found me.

This is a love letter.

It's dedicated to those whose spirits have been haunted, and whose hearts have been left empty and broken by the physical and emotional abuses of the church, only to be thrown out like rotting garbage in a dumpster so as not to spoil the rest of the "good fruit" by the very same evangelical fundamentalist community that once called you a friend in Christ. It's dedicated to the restless souls tormented by the plaguing thoughts of spending an eternity in hell and the loss of one's faith and hope in finding inner peace in this life or the next. Its dedicated to the users and the used of society that have tried drinking ,snorting, injecting anything and everything in the futile attempts to kill the pain and silence the voices of sin's shame, guilt and despair erstwhile sinking further into a downward spiral of addiction. It's dedicated to those who have lost their faith and to all the things we try to do to numb the pain and all shit we put ourselves through to escape the self –hate, rejection, and the feeling of self-worthlessness that drives us to our own isolation and eventually insanity. It's dedicated to the Christian who has lost friends and family members, after leaving the church because they no longer could accept the premise that using eternal damnation as a path to eternal love is not only not credible but actually contradicts the very essence and definition of agape love. And because of their decision to leave the church they found their self-identity shattered standing at the edge of an unknown void.

- Brent Brumbaugh

THE BEGINNING

There is a secret place in the farthest corners of my memory that comes to me in the delicate light of early spring. It's a place where the wisps of magic and eternal mystery wait for me in that breath between sleep and wake. It speaks to me in a tongue not known by grown men, the language of a child's imagination. It is a pure state that is so hard to hold onto, like the slipping away of a perfect sunset as your eyes try to steal the vision and make it their own, or the taste of your first kiss as it fleets in a bloom of innocent emotion.

It's a feeling that I have right now and it reminds me of everything that life should be.
I remember gathering Easter eggs in my green and yellow striped long sleeve shirt. It was Easter day and our family was in a state of perfection, at least in my child like recollection. The earth was a warm and safe place and my

home was its center.

Before the complications of sexuality, politics, death and destruction all over the world, there was green grass, mom's Sunday dress and my dad in his stylish solid white, 3-piece suit. To me, these were the visions of innocence and purity. I remember looking up at my eggshell white house and seeing the bees balancing on the rhododendron flowers. The air smelled of fresh cut grass accompanied by the distant whirring and grumbling of the neighbors' lawn mowers.

My childhood dog, Thorin (named after the heroic dwarf from The Hobbit) was a massive black and white brindle patterned Great Dane.
I rode him like a horse as a child and enjoyed his loving playfulness. Despite his strength and ability to cause immense injury to an intruder, he was extremely gentle with me and allowed me to rough house with him in the way that very young children do; twisting noses and sticking hands in his mouth, getting covered in drool and rolling around in the dirt and grass.

Before the advent of controllers for the television, I was the willful recipient of the nickname, "R.C." which stood for remote control. When we were together, especially when with my older brother and sister, I was commissioned with changing the channels on the television. This was the dawn of the color TV era. A time when MTV was just beginning and HBO was a channel of pure sin and secret delight to us kids. Madonna was Desperately Seeking Susan and Michael Jackson was at the height of his coolness. Despite these cultural events and their influences, we were a devout Christian family who attended Life Center in Tacoma. Life Center was one of the first of a new kind of church that would be copied and replicated throughout America and the world. It was a mega-church with the largest following in the Pacific Northwest at the time of our attendance.

Pastor Fulton Buntain was a Canadian transplant that had made the church into a thriving meeting place for many Christians in the area. The church complex boasted a full elementary and high school, a senior center and a food bank.

My mother had come from a Lutheran background and liked the Assemblies of God brand of Christianity that was preached at Life Center. My father had grown up in a Mormon household, which benefited greatly from the assistance that the Mormon Church had provided during the hard times they went through during his own childhood. My older brother and sister were related to me through my mother's first marriage. The three of us kids all grew up in what many would deem to be an idyllic setting except for the frequent complaint that I, as the baby of the family was given more than they as the elder siblings had received.

One of my first memories was our vacation to Disneyland and Universal Studios where I picked up a prop van and later was terrified by the "Jaws" adventure tram in which the huge mechanical shark sprung out from the water with its monstrous jaws snapping at me.

Not long after Disneyland, I spent an evening with my mother watching the Billy Graham crusade on television. At the time, an event like this was still a pretty common sight during Sunday night prime time. When I heard the words of Billy Graham, they were like the words of a stately grandfather, speaking to me the eternal truths of life in a way that I as a very young child could still understand.

He spoke about the absolute love of Jesus Christ and his assuming of all the sins of the world onto himself as a sacrifice to God the Father on the world's behalf. I was very little and full of the kind of wonder that only a child can possess.

This message, though I had heard it in passing had captured my attention in a deep and powerful way. I turned to my mother and told her that I wanted to give my heart to Jesus and she proudly led me through the steps as Billy guided with his own words what I should say. I spoke the words and called in to the crusade to report my conversion. During the call to salvation, the soft and warm hymn arose from the stadium crowd:

"Just as I am without one plea, but that thy blood was shed for me.
And as thou bids me, 'come to me', oh Lamb of God, I come, I come."

As a gift, they sent me a small red New Testament Bible. From that time on, I took my faith in Jesus and the words of the Bible very seriously. I remember getting up with a heart full of passion in front of my family, using our fireplace keep as my own little platform, asking them to please turn with me to the first chapter of 1982. I rained hellfire and brimstone; I spoke with fury and verve about the transformative power of a relationship with Jesus and the illumination of the Holy Spirit in a would-be lost life. I mimicked the ways and mannerisms of Jimmy Swaggart, whom my mother also liked because he was the cousin of Jerry Lee Lewis.

No matter where I went, or what I did, I was a little missionary for Jesus. During one of those early summers, our family traveled to Salt Lake City, Utah to pass out tracts and propaganda that showed Mormons the error of Mormonism and the truths of our brand of Protestantism. We were a part of the ex-Mormon group known as Saints Alive, or Ex-Mormons for Jesus. Mormonism's public enemy #1, Ed Decker, headed this ministry. Ed had written a book called, "The God Makers" in which he catalogued his personal testimony of Jesus saving him from Mormonism. The details of the way the Mormon Church operated shocked many Christians and converted many Mormons to our version of Christianity. Though Mormons had some terrible things to say about Ed, I knew him well and loved him and his wife Carol like an Aunt and Uncle.

To this day, I still remain in friendship with their youngest son, Josh and care for the Decker family a great deal. I remember that first trip to Utah for many of its strange and wonderful sights; members of our group dragging a life sized cross around the outer perimeter of the Mormon Temple in downtown Salt Lake City, the tracts I handed out with their blue skies and soul-redeeming information, the smell of the desert air in the summer breeze. This was a natural extension of all that I believed and it filled my heart with a sense that I, at my young age was already storing up for myself a great deal of treasure in heaven.

I was a part of a small, but faithful group of true believers who were on a mission to save the lost and bring them to Jesus. We were there to help those already in confusion about who the true Jesus was to a more accurate understanding of the Bible and proper theology.

Where other children had difficulty in grasping the basics of evangelical Christian doctrine, my passion and heart to not see a single soul sent to hell gave me a ferocity rarely seen in a child towards learning such heady adult topics of spirituality. Somehow, it was as natural to me as riding on my big wheel, or playing with G.I. Joes. This natural talent and spiritual attenuation was a two edged sword; on one hand, I tried to behave myself because I wanted to serve Jesus even when nobody was watching, but on the other hand, I had terrible nightmares and events that are on the cusp of my memory that bordered on what can best be described as demonic.

To me, it was like the devil knew that I was going to be a great warrior for God and wanted to stop me in some way. The thought of being a spiritual warrior in training was an allegorical concept frequently used in my Sunday school and helped me have a coping device when these strange and murky dreams and visions of evil would come to me.

In one of my most memorable reoccurring events, an evil owl would be walking in heavy sand towards me, making a horrible stomping sound like the shaking of large metal buckets full of ball bearings. The ominous spiritual nausea filled me with a frequent uneasiness. I referred to this and other apparitions as "the stompers" and told my parents about it. They decided that the evil spirits had used an antique Buddha statue as a demonic gateway into our otherwise hedged home and threw it out.

Though the stompers never returned, the harassment of my dreams and imagination by malevolent forces never went away. I was told that to call on Jesus, or to specifically say the words, "I rebuke you in the name of Jesus!" would make the apparitions leave me alone. Even so, there was many a night that I spent while the rest of the house was asleep, waiting for the devil to confront me. So I did what any child in the situation of facing the dark angel of hell would do, I slept between my mattress and the wall to allow as little of myself for him to grab as possible.

When I woke up, a new day awaited and I faced it with a cheerfulness and odd sense of humor that is still a part of mc today. I attended the elementary school at Life Center, as my older brother and sister had done as well. We had the benefit of a private education in our earlier years because of the steady pay my father received from his work as a commercial graphic artist at the Boeing Corporation. Life Christian, as it was called, indeed provided a top-notch education by any respect, with the addition of Pentecostal doctrine. Church services and events were a part of the curriculum at Life Christian and were normal to me.

My friends in the neighborhood who attended public school had very strange stories that were totally alien to me. It was as if they always had a secret that they didn't want to tell me because I was "safety boy". I earned this nickname with acts of extreme piety. Most prominent among these acts was the magazine incident: I remember coming up to the guys huddled around something that I could not see from a distance.

As I got closer, I realized it was a porn magazine that somebody had just left on the street. A wave of boyish curiosity washed over me; to see a woman naked, bare breasted and displayed for my pleasure was as foreign to me as Russian furniture assembly instructions. As I drew closer, I felt sin calling me to dive in and hide it away, to keep it for my own. It was my forbidden fruit and I understood how sweet that fruit could taste. As the guys let me in to have a look as well, a shudder of righteousness coursed through me and I grabbed the magazine with my eyes closed and ripped it to shreds. Never did so much emotion come to me in every direction at that young age as it did then. The fear, flickers of innocent curiosity, the shame of letting down my friends and the regret of tearing up something I desired to experience so badly.

I ran home crying while the guys picked up the shreds to look at the jigsaw puzzle that I had left them. When I told my mother what had happened, she told me I had done the right thing and my emotions slowed to a mellow sense of vindication of being in the wrong. The kids in the neighborhood and I always had good times playing every day after school. Despite my unfortunate nickname, I surprised the other kids more than once with my daredevil moves, jumping over fences from the tops of garage roofs and climbing high into the trees. One day, while my friend, Corey and I sat and played in my sandbox, I told him the whole story of the Gospel. Between scoops of sand, I spoke about the creation of the earth as an expression of God's love for us and the betrayal of that utopia by the first sin of Adam and Eve, aided by the cunning serpent, the devil.

As our plastic trucks crashed together, I told Corey about the fall of man and the exile we all have all been cursed to by the original sin that Adam and Eve committed. With conviction and a face covered in dirt and snot, I told him about how the only way to redeem us from this fallen state was to give ourselves wholly to Jesus and ask him into our heart. I explained that Jesus had taken all of Corey's sins from him and put them upon himself along with those of the rest of the world and paid the debt of sin with his own self-sacrifice. As we took our shoes off and poured out the sand that had collected as we played, I asked Corey if he would say a prayer to Jesus with me and he did.

At that moment, I felt the spark of hope for the

entire world, that I myself could somehow turn the tide of evil by sharing the gospel of Jesus Christ to the entire world, just as the Bible had commissioned me. I felt like I was a young disciple with much to contribute to the kingdom of heaven. I believed it wholeheartedly and thought in these terms. These feelings and thoughts were nurtured and encouraged.

At Saints Alive meetings, I would often be surrounded by dozens of adults who would discuss doctrine and plans for the organization. I would often be the only child there, with Optimus Prime, G.I. Joe and Jesus Christ. Many of those dear hearted people were very kind to me, especially Sally, who constantly promised that I would be a great servant of the kingdom of God. I remember her kind face as she told me that I would greet kings and people in high places. Sally was always one to encourage me, to the satisfaction of my mother and father.

My Father was a man that I held in high esteem and was my archetype for God; stately, hard at work, often distant or detached, but loving. The way I perceived him in the years of my youth worked perfectly with the biblical styling of the one true God. My mother was warm and endearing to the point of extreme corniness. She had a difficult life of her own, with a happy upbringing until the passing of her father. Even then, I perceived a deep hurt that never seemed to lift from her. In my early years, I clung to her and came to her as she often called for big hugs and warm snuggles.

I was too young to understand the intricacies of adult emotion, or the concerns of my caretakers and nurturers. The greatest complication and source of hurt and bitterness came from an accident that occurred before I was born.

My father was driving a small Fiat sedan and went to take a left hand turn that appeared to be clear. But before anything could be done, the car collided with a Buick estate station wagon that was traveling at 50 MPH. The impact on the little car flipped, hurled and crushed it onto my mother's side.

My mother was ashen, unconscious and bleeding from her mouth. My father, a Vietnam veteran medic, knew this to be a deadly sign. My older sister-to-be was lost, being carried by my mother and having taken the brunt of the impact on the little Fiat. My mother was thought to be dead, only to be revived later by the medics. During this time, my mother says she traveled from her body to heaven, bathed in unfathomable light and love in the presence of God. In this rapturous moment, the almighty told her that her time was not over on earth, that her purpose was unfulfilled and that she was to return. Just like that she returned from heaven and into a world of pain from a crushed pelvis and collapsed lungs.

My family was in absolute sadness after the accident. This was the world I came into on August 14th, 1977. I was born just 13 months after the accident that took my sister-to-be. When I was old enough to hear, I was told that I was a child of promise and hope, a child that healed the family's pain. As a small child, that is exactly what I did and my mother clung to me with warmth, love and affection.

I don't discount my mother's death experience and believe her story exactly as she tells it. It is her life and story, not mine. However, in my studies, I have discovered that it is common for religious people to have near death experiences featuring their patron saint, or God. Her vision of God is contrasted by those of other faiths seeing the Virgin Mary, Buddha, Allah and countless other deities during near death experiences. Raymond Moody published a book, Life After LIfe, which compiled studies with people who had Near Death Experiences

(NDE's). This was the first of its kind, documenting these experiences. There are many more books now published on the subject that are worth reading.

At ten years old, I was given the opportunity to take part in a missionary adventure called "Kings Kids". Kings Kids was a YWAM sponsored missionary trip that used the cuteness of kids in song and dance routines as a method of spreading the gospel into otherwise inhospitable places. In my case, our trip was to China, the Philippines and Macau.

This was the single most life-changing event of my young life, as it showed me that there was more to the world than just my American life. I participated with sincerity and absolute joy that I was sharing the good news of the gospel to people who were "lost in the darkness". This was the first time I was away from my parents and it felt like some sort of spiritual rite of passage. I turned 11 years old on the S.S. Shanghai in the South China Sea, stricken with a nasty flu bug.

Fast forward to my teen years, I changed from private school to Stadium High. This was the school that my older brother and sister attended and was made famous by the film, "Ten Things I Hate About You". I was unaware of the shelter I was leaving when I began classes. I was a scrawny, doe eyed kid wearing a shirt depicting Jesus bloodily bench-pressing the cross in an emulation of "Gold's Gym", instead saying "Lord's Gym...His pain, your gain". Let's just say the metal heads in wood shop found me particularly easy to pick on.

I discovered wonderful things like girls and pornography and pot, but always struggled with my faith versus my desire to know and see more about these new and exciting things. By this point, my big brother was a police officer and my sister was married to a minister in training. Law and order surrounded me, as it seemed.

I attended a church in which my brother in law was the Jr. High minister's assistant and went to their Wednesday youth group. The high school pastor was a Chicago transplant named Herman. A large and joyful black man who played music and got everybody charged up about Jesus. I will share more on this fellow later on.

So my high school experience was peppered with equal parts guilt, excitement and adventure, but I always remained solid in my base beliefs. I was, after all the most knowledgeable in matters of the quotation of biblical verse.

Upon graduation I began attending a local college. This was short lived, as I was disinterested in getting a degree just for the sake of it. In the 3rd quarter of my first year I dropped out. I moved in with my friend Charles and began working in Seattle at a sporting goods factory. The work was tedious and unexciting, but I utilized all my spare time reading the Bible cover to cover. My brother in law became the high school pastor at a very small church in Olympia, WA, a significant bus ride from Tacoma. Being young and full of excitement for ministry, I volunteered to help out with the youth group.

The pastor of the small church suggested I attend a theology school in Seattle and offered to assist me in getting in. I was accepted and moved to Seattle to begin my studies. The environment was a mixture of devout biblical study and fervor for Holy Ghost revival. Now that I had a motivating subject of interest, I went on to study for the next 3 years. During that time, I married my college girlfriend and began playing in Christian rock bands. There were moments in College that are so funny to me even now, like trying to masturbate in a room full of other guys in the middle of the night, knowing that they were also waiting to quietly do the same without anyone knowing.

It even became a bit of a game, seeing who could bust another for the sin of masturbation. To us, it was serious and not acceptable behavior. I remember the feeling of accomplishment I felt after I hadn't masturbated in over a month, but then the sinning continued.

It was also a big concern within the school to keep us couples from running off and fornicating somewhere, so they held strict curfews, even for single men as old as 45. That of course didn't keep any of us from giving in to the sin of fornication with our girlfriends. I cannot explain the enormous struggle it was to be in my early 20's and feeling like the act of sex was punishable by hell. This brought me to guilty tears on many an occasion, feeling like I was betraying God with my filth. If I were to sin regularly in this way, then I was certainly rejecting the salvation that Christ offered me in exchange for cheap and unholy thrills outside of the marriage bed. But life went on and my studies continued. I really took to playing music and participating in the worship team, even writing some worship songs myself. The school was like a safe bubble of idyllic Christian utopia, stuffed in the gentrified corner of Seattle known as Ballard.

By the third year, my interest in playing in a Christian rock band full time came to the forefront of my plans. With our first child on the way, I moved with my band to Nashville, TN. For my young wife and I, this move represented to us a great leap of faith; faith that, from our perspective, few others had. We were doing the good work of spreading the gospel through the thinly veiled cloak of rock music.

Here in this environment, I learned a great many things, foremost of which was that our unbridled faith gave us the boldness to do things that could be construed as foolish. I don't want to discount the experience though, because the sum of all my experiences has made me the man I am today. That being said, the Nashville venture turned out to be a bad idea. Once my son was born and my wife recovered, we decided to return to Seattle.

Still excited to make a living in music, I formed a new group with some good friends of mine and began playing local clubs in Seattle. We gained a decent amount of success and toured nationally. After 3 years of touring, scraping by and seeing the birth of my daughter I was ready to give up on my dream of being a messianic rock star and went back to finish my last year in college.

I returned to college in Seattle for my final year, but I had grown, matured and developed a healthy suspicion over my faith. I started to see the holes that I had glossed over for all my life. I started seeing the insanity that was acceptable, because it was for Christ. My worldview was changing and no matter how hard I tried to fight it, I was losing my faith.

I will cover the details of the faith loss experience later on, but I would like to convey the amazing amount of fear, anxiety and pain that this feeling causes. To leave my faith, to disavow Christ, to walk away was to doom myself to hell if I was wrong about my feelings. Heavy stuff.

At that time, I was finishing up my last year in college and frequenting a pizza place across the street from the school. One of the main cats who worked there was a guy who went by the name of Steve. He and I would often have feisty debates over the meaning of life and the universe. Ask anyone who knew me during that time and they will tell you that I certainly knew my way around a Bible. I was always stumped by Steve's unshakable faith in the chaos that comes from mystery. What I mean is, he was ok with NOT having the answers to every question, he was ok with not knowing what tomorrow held. At the time, this was a mind-blowing concept because as an evangelical Christian, I had all my bases covered, my answers well rehearsed and my ducks in a row. Sure, I didn't "feel" God in the way I was supposed to as a Christian, but I felt quite confident about where I stood. Steve and I chatted on and on until he talked about the idea that we're just "floating in the universe" without any purpose being necessary. You see, my faith system at the time was fear and ego driven; hell was real and Jesus loved me and set me aside as his delightful thing even though he created such an awful place. During those conversations with Steve, something began to change in me, it started to resonate with me that I wasn't the center of the universe, but just a part of the world and a singular person among billions. Enough other details in my studies had been nagging at me as well, to the point where I no longer believed in the concept of Christianity.

After years of putting my family through the ringer with our musical travels and attempts to make it all work, coupled with my change of worldview, my relationship with my wife became nearly non-existent. By the time I graduated, I had split up with my wife and found a girlfriend.

I was a man without a center, an anchor, any grounding. I was a balloon escaping from a child's hand, growing smaller and smaller as I climbed into the clear blue sky. Everything in my life went into total upheaval, and like anyone who has gone through a change that big, I went a little nuts for a while.

I found myself walking down a dirty industrial road in Seattle, feeling like every step was a metaphor for what I was and who I had become. The cold wind, the filthy rain soaked sidewalk, the passing cars and my loneliness all singing in chorus to the tune of a dismal town that's made to crush dreams. If anyone had told me what I would accomplish in the next few years, I would have had a hard time believing it. Ever since I left the security of my former faith, everything else seemed sad, bleak and surreal. I knew that facts were facts and that perhaps I was just a drop of water in the sea of humanity, but that ache for the idea of unconditional love and what it brings made me so recklessly messy. I tried to pour my new and untested views on love and redemption into my new girlfriend, but what could really be expected from a freshly separated 27-year-old

man and a 19 year old girl fresh out of rehab?
Trouble.
So began the dark year.

THE GOSPEL

From the moment we first realize our existence, we naturally find ourselves asking the questions, "Who am I? What is all this about? Do I have a purpose?" These questions have been asked by our ancestors and have been subject to every possible answer under the sun, but few answers so keenly compare to the basic idea of the gospel. God loved the world, but the world was full of sin, so a sacrifice needed to be made to pay for the debt of evil in order to restore our standing with him. God sent his only son as the ultimate sacrifice for you and I and all we need to do is to restore this separation from God is to accept the sacrifice given and live a life that honors the Son of God.

To many of you who may read this, this story changed your life. You became transformed by the idea that God, the maker of heaven and earth wants communion with you and wants you to dwell with him in heaven for all eternity.
I know a man who was lost in the throes of a desperate addiction to crack cocaine. When the

gospel came to him, he was utterly broken, his will surrendered, his mindset so completely and instantaneously changed that he never touched the pipe again. I know innumerable stories like his in which the transformative power of the story of the gospel took people and turned them around and they have never looked back. This is a real thing, a true experience and a mind-altering event that turns sinners to saints. It is not the kind of event that you look back at like a trip to Disneyland, or a pretty sunset, it is a moment that you relive. Salvation and the memory of this story that you believe with all of your heart are repeated in your mind on a daily basis. Christ died for me, so I will daily live for him.

The New Testament, home of the four gospels of Matthew, Mark, Luke and John is full of reminders, stories and examples of what this sacrifice should mean to you and how you should live to honor it. There is no other major religion that puts so much weight on a singular experience quite in the way that Christianity puts on salvation. No matter what argument is made, no matter how grand some other story is, it cannot compare to "The Greatest Story Ever Told". When this experience sinks in, you change entirely. The immense commission given to you to live daily for Christ dwarfs your old motivations and aspirations.

At such a young age, I swallowed the gospel whole and ran with it. I thought myself lucky to have been given a head start on living a life for Christ and not seeing the terrible marks that sin and depravity ravage the world by.

When people asked me who I was in a spiritual sense, I could always reply with confidence: I am a slave to Christ and a child of God, vouchsafed for an inheritance that my father in heaven has for me when I die. I knew what life was about: Life is an expression of the love story that God wrote for us, ending in an eternity of joy in heaven. I knew my purpose: My purpose is to spread the good news of God's love and salvation to everyone so that they too may live with him in heaven for all eternity. Once this was my mindset and there was a clear purpose given to me through the Holy Scriptures. It was the coolest thing in the world to me; nothing else compared to the value of this realization in my life. When you become saved, you accept Jesus into your heart. Jesus Christ is now living in your heart!

In my mind, Jesus had a front row seat to my daily life and watched over me with protection and love. My every decision was led and directed by the Holy Spirit, giving me confidence in my path of righteousness. I felt like whatever I did was somehow predetermined and set within the safe harbor of Christ's guidance.

Life was not banal and dry, but full of energy and mystic adventure! It was the thing that kept me going on days when I felt bad about my situation, my failures, and myself. With Jesus sitting upon the throne of my heart, everything was different. It was as if I was looking through the rosy shades of the sacrifice of Jesus Christ, which showed me the world in his perspective.

When I looked out on the condition of the world, I saw the madness that the sin the world embraced had unleashed pain and suffering on humanity. With my crimson stained set of eyes my Christian perspective automatically drove my politics and opinions. I was ravenous in my studies and relentless in my thirst to learn more. Despite the difficulty and near impossible nature of reading the Bible in its entirety, I took this task upon myself, thinking of myself as the most devout among all of my peers and certainly more so than most fully grown adults. In this state, I personified the idea that the Bible is the only book anyone really needed to read, for it held the words of Salvation.

From an outsiders perspective, this seems close-minded crazy-talk, but to the initiate, the Bible is the only book on earth which, though written by over 40 authors in 3 languages over hundreds of years, was congruently guided by the hand of God.

Within the Bible, I found the history of the earth told. Our past, present and future state are all laid out and woven beautifully together. The Bible was explained to me as the story of the gospel; every story is an allegory and a foreshadowing of Christ. If after Christ's death and resurrection, it is a further explanation of the mysteries of God's eternal plan. Because the whole Bible is an intricate story of humanity's salvation, the tone and texture of the gospel become equally more complex. A lifetime of study of the Bible in our English language is enough to satiate a hungry mind for a lifetime, should one be up for the task and I was excited to be such a person.

However, as I studied, I came across a conundrum, on one hand, the gospel is quite simple: We were bad and couldn't make up for it, so God made up for it for us so we could be with him. On the other hand: Christ did die for you as the ultimate sacrifice, but to live life and just say "thanks buddy!" to God and go about your business unchanged is an insult to the sacrifice made for your sake. Therefore, we have some ground rules to abide by. What those ground rules are is unclear at times since there are volumes and volumes of rules that the Israelites had to abide by, which we should probably adhere to, yet seem impractical in this day and age. The Ten Commandments are the foundation of the Judeo-Christian faith and should be adhered to, but Jesus said the only rules are to love God with all your heart and love your neighbor as you love yourself. Conversely, the apostle Paul has a few new things to add to that list. You should not eat meat that has been sacrificed to idols of false gods unless you don't know it was sacrificed to the aforementioned gods.

Well, you can if you want to, but not if it offends your fellow Christians who participated in these former false religions and think it wrong. Jesus came to save the Jews, but a grace has been extended to all humanity so that everyone can get in on the bargain. Though, Christ's sacrifice was all encompassing, Jesus said to save another man was to cover for a multitude of sins. So if this is the case, it's unclear why that would be necessary. It's really like having two forms of health insurance, except this is anti-hell insurance. Homosexuality is wrong because the Old Testament text speaks of men not laying with men as they would lay with a woman, but Jesus is silent on the matter, but the apostle Paul says sodomites will not be allowed into the kingdom of heaven. Paul also says that we could stay living in our old ways, but it would be like carrying a dead corpse on your back what with the "old man" abiding with the "new man". Then there's the grey area of whether or not we actually have free will, or if our life is like a movie in which our fates have been set since the beginning of time, unchangeable and immovable. Again, Paul says that some "vessels" are made for destruction and others are meant to be filled and used properly. This is an allegory for the idea that people going to hell may be sent there just to show the people not going to hell just how good they have it!

What I had come across was a disparity between the basic gospel and the intellectual gospel. At first, It was only spoon fed the "milk" of the gospel and later would be introduced to the much more complex and seemingly conflicted "meat" of the gospel.

A presently devout Christian may take partiality with my depiction of what the gospel really is, but enough study of the Bible makes this paradoxical stumbling block quite clear. What I was really looking at was the fine print of the salvation contract and the fine print that we end up reading after signing up. When all these complexities and rules that faded to shades of gray mounted up to the point of mental overkill, I simply would put my Bible down and remember that: "Jesus loves me, this I know. For the Bible tells me so."

Among all this chatter between which of these two gospels is the real one, I found myself clinging to the most child-like of thoughts. Those songs that Christian children sing reinforce the idea that the love of God is readily available to them. This reinforcement was the super glue that held my faith together and still holds the "saved" together in times of trouble.

This dichotomy was the thing that allowed my Christian mind to accept big truths and overlook the grey areas. Avoiding these disparities helped me to keep on keeping on with the good vibes that the first salvation experience gave me. Splitting hairs over doctrine was a staple of the more advanced Christian, but it came with the craggy difficulties of fractured thought. I felt that I was an advanced Christian and as such had an inside scoop to the real meaning of it all, but that knowledge weighed down on my heart with the dark turmoil of a seeker whose teacher says opposing things in the same breath.

Some may wonder how it is possible for the Gospel to be at one point so transformative, but self-contradictory. I was one who felt this way. It was a struggle burning in my mind that created a fire of discontentment and confusion. I had to at some point conclude that the reason the Gospel seemed contradictory, or full of unseen terms and conditions was because that was indeed the case. The basic gospel concept of a loving god saving us from doom is a common idea among non-Christians. For example, I think many non-Christians would say they believe this statement: God is love and therefore loves the entire world. Despite the evil in the world we can experience the real love that is God in an endless number of ways.

I finally came to the conclusion that the Gospel changes minds and hearts because we all want to be loved by God. When we hear a story that tells us that God loves us, we take it!
Right here and now as I write, I fully believe that God loves me and wants communion with me. How that really occurs and what catalyst is involved is where I differ from the Gospel that the Bible lays out. This is where we all are. My friend who used to smoke crack lived in a world where he was not loved, where drugs were the

only things he could take to feel good. The goodness that he felt from drugs was temporary and it was not love. When we grow up in abuse or neglect, when we are ugly and unwanted, when we want to be held and are not, we are hungering for the one thing we cannot seem to grasp: love.

The gospel takes us to a place where we feel loved by an unchanging, eternal and good source. If we are alone, God is in our hearts loving us. When we fail, God loves and forgives us. In any scenario possibly imaginable, we have the love of God. The question is whether this version of the story is really the truth, or what we happened to hear. If you grew up hearing, "God is love and therefore loves the entire world. Despite the evil in the world, we can experience the real love that is God in an endless number of ways." Do you think that you would need to hear a story that included a blood sacrifice and the threat of Hell? I don't think you would. Why would you? It would be like deciding between getting free tacos vs. getting free tacos and having to see somebody die for your free tacos. Nobody would choose that.

After my 20+ years of devoted study, I have concluded that the gospel is a beautiful and transformative story; one that has some fine print that some will never read into. In the end, the gospel may be the best version of God's love story that some will ever hear. For that reason alone I believe it can be a good thing for some people. But the blood and guts of it, mixed with an eternal hell to punish those who do not accept puts people into an unhealthy mindset in which such violent things on an eternal scale are permissible and a necessary part of life.

SHARING THE GOOD NEWS

Jesus gave believers a statement known as the Great Commission, in Matthew 28:18-20 (NIV): Then Jesus came to them and said, "All authority in heaven and on earth has been given to me. Therefore go and make disciples of all nations, baptizing them in the name of the Father and of the Son and of the Holy Spirit, and teaching them to obey everything I have commanded you. And surely I am with you always, to the very end of the age."

This is the foundation of what is required of every good Christian. It is often something that new Christians already want to do, so it works out. When you are a new believer, you see the whole world as a dark and dismal place that desperately needs the transformative power of the gospel in the hearts of every living man and woman. For more than two decades, this was the case in my mind; I couldn't help but feel a sense of compassion for those in darkness.

When I was a child, this was often on the

forefront of my mind, both because at church and school I was told of the urgency of spreading the gospel and because of the good nature of my child-self. Ultimately, it was a heavy-handed message that my Christian school and church pounded into me. I was distressed at such brutal ideas of my friends burning in Hell. In these institutions, I was asked questions like, "You don't want your friends to burn in hell, do you?" and "Who will take up the call to bring the lost to salvation?" I sat there, thinking that what these adults told me was the wholehearted truth, worrying about my friends and the ones I loved who were not clear Christian believers and I truly fretted for there souls...at six years old!

At such a young age and without any form of critical thinking or intellectual skills really capable of tackling such a monumental subject as the fate of one's ever-living soul, I happily accepted the call to bring others to salvation. When I applied this, I gave Corey my sand box sermon and converted him. I had done nothing wrong; I had done the most right I had ever done. I had led Corey "to the Lord!"

Corey was only the first of my young evangelical endeavors. Before the age of ten years old, I had led numerous neighborhood children "to the Lord" and wore this fact as a badge of honor. I was doing what I was told, what was the truth, what was the mandate of my unshakable faith!

I imagine some of you might read this and think how bat-shit-crazy this sounds, while others might look at this and say that I started out with such promise, but "fell away" from the Lord and have been now misled into perdition and all manner of wickedness. It's funny how good minds can think so differently. To the outsider looking in, Christianity is a culture-ruining blight upon the diversity and beauty of all the aspects of humanity, a scourge of false righteousness and blind sighted Theocratic cliché. It is hard to defend this outsiders view, because the spreading of the Gospel takes traditions that go back thousands of years, throws them by the wayside and replaces them with the homogenized western story of Christianity.

At ten years old, I went to China, The Philippines and South Korea with the performing arts group, "Kings Kids". Good family friends, Tom and Cindy, led this group that would travel around the world, performing, smuggling bibles where they were illegal in children's clothing and spreading the gospel quietly in the Chinese Christian underground network.
Despite my present feelings that these practices

we mortifyingly unethical, I would like to make perfectly clear that these people were good to the core and had the best of intentions doing what they believed was right. In their minds, they were nothing short of secret agents for the Almighty.

My international missionary experience provided me with an example of what real warriors for Christ are willing to do. This mindset became the foundation for my cemented confidence in the truth and power of the gospel. I was able to sing and dance for children who lived in garbage dumps and perform at national monuments in China, including the Great Wall. I had converted grown men to Christianity, I had seen the devastation and suppression from godless Chinese governmental rule, I was a part of the mission, one that others were too afraid to do. All of these experiences reinforced my view that the gospel was a worldwide phenomenon that I was a part of. I was a child on the front lines in the battle for the soul of mankind; I was a devout, super-elite-ninja of the gospel!

When I returned home, I was buzzing with pious optimism and energy. To have traveled across the world to save a soul from hell was an indescribably blissful accomplishment that I had earned. There is no feeling like being fully in the belief that you are instrumental in the most powerful and freeing experience any human can experience. Helping restore humanity to a right and proper relationship with the maker of all of the heavens and the earth was my task, and one that I would aspire to make a living from.

In college, my primary goal was to become educated in the ways of missionary work. Seattle Bible College had proudly produced hundreds of pastors and missionaries over the decades of its existence. There were many good-hearted people who had devoted a lifetime of work for the sake of the gospel and continued this work by teaching the next generation in the ways of ministry. One of these people was Ned; a charming and wacky elderly man who had graduated from our school in the 1950's and established himself as a missionary to the remote regions of southern Mexico. He was an expert in the ancient Greek texts of the Bible and was passionate and kind to the core.

One of the most moving stories he told me was that he had fallen ill with amoebic dysentery and was very sick, too sick to leave his bed. He had however committed himself to go speak at a small church in a small town and felt the Lord telling him that he had to go. So he got into his car and drove the hour and a half drive to this remote village. He stumbled into the church and got up to speak, and just as he went to speak, he felt better! To me this was yet another proof that the good news needed to be told and God would sustain those who are bold enough to forsake everything to follow his will. There was, however a very sharp contrast to Ned, he held to the letter of the Greek part of the Bible in such a manner that he felt it very strongly about people learning it and understanding what was really being said. Through his evidence, he made a very convincing case for the more complex version of the gospel as I laid out in the previous chapter. It was a thin line between heaven and hell, even if you claimed to be a Christian. In this scenario of biblical hair splitting, you were a KFC chicken and God was Colonel Saunders...and he was hungry!

Ned's biggest point was, If the Bible is the word of God, then we better make sure that we really know what He is saying and follow it to the letter! There is no excuse in claiming ignorance, for we were given the knowledge of God in our hearts. The lost were truly doomed and even the halfway Christians were heading to hell. There was no fudging or glazing over parts of the Bible we didn't like or agree with. It was take it or leave it, whole thing or hell. Frankly speaking, if you were to accept the validity of the Bible, as we know it to be the inerrant word of God, this should be the case. After all, this is God's word we are talking about, right? Ned thumbed his nose at the popular motivational speaker type of preaching that pervaded the evangelical circles and had the doctrinal prowess to back it up. In a world where the good news was milk, Ned was fully capable of parsing the words in the original Greek to provide those elite of us the meat of doctrine. The unfortunate part of this realist approach was that it greatly increased the hell bound body count. But who are we to challenge God? The answer created a very clear-cut decision for me: Accept the whole bible as is without partiality or exception, or reject the word of God and fall into perdition.

I would challenge any Christian who has dug deep into the heavy details of the original language of the New Testament to show me that this doctrinal viewpoint is not true. The reality is that the good news is a humanitarian nightmare. I found myself in tears, knowing the impossible statistics of people over all of human history who would, by the lion's share be carted off into an eternal abyss of fiery torture by my God of love. The fact is, Christianity at its fundamental core forces you to accept the reality of hell and make you accept it as ok because God is God and can do whatever he pleases. It turns out that the good news is only good news for a chosen few who are capable of maintaining their faith until their final days; otherwise, they too are doomed.

In the real meat and potatoes of the Gospels and other New Testament text, there is no room for laid back Christianity or "greasy grace" as we called it. I now understood that if people were not up for the mental gymnastics of the fine print of the good news, they wouldn't make the spiritual cut either.

This was the kind of thing that really made me wonder how this could be true. Not only was it bad enough that so many people had to go to hell because their impurity was not washed away by the blood of Christ, but the fine print showed that a much more elite group was really only worthy of heaven. I started to wonder if the God that I had grown to love and worship and pray to was really capable of this emotionally upsetting contest of sin and salvation.

With all of this in mind, I eventually came to the realization that the good news is actually the story of a God who makes a contest for who is good enough. Yes, salvation is freely given according to the Bible, but has a real eternal cost if not abided by. I can best explain it in the following parable:

A great and rich father had ten children. He knew that he would be busy with his own affairs and did not have time to attend to the needs of his children. He was a pure and pious man, of perfect reputation and regard. He collected his children to him at a very young age and told them, "My children, I am great and pure and so too may you be. I will give you all that I have upon a later time of my choosing. Here I have laid out my conditions and plans in this holy document. I will be gone and you will not see me until I return, at a time that you will least expect me.

If I find that you have loved me and followed my conditions until my return, I shall give you all that I have just as I promised. However, if I find that you have not heeded my direction, but have done poorly and shamed me in any way, I will return at a time, which you least expect me and will dowse you in gasoline and set you on fire. I do not wish for this to be so, but I am pure and you may be too if you abide under the wings of my mercy and goodness, living under the conditions that I have laid out to you. Until the time of my return, you will not see me, but may speak to me into the wind and I will hear.

You may not hear my response, but I will have sent it if you listen hard enough. I am leaving you now, do as I have said and you will avoid my punishment and inherit all that I have promised you." He then left his children to their own devices with his document of instruction on purity and was not seen or heard from for a seemingly endless time. The children grew and became men and women of both good and ill refute, some having heeded their father's words and others ignoring him, claiming him to be an absentee father who was impossible to please. But a day came in which the father returned to find his children in all walks of life and doing a great many things.

He came upon each of them at a time they did not expect and found all but one to have eventually disregarded his document of instructions. He bound them and dowsed them in gasoline, ignoring their cries for mercy or forgiveness. "I am sorry, that time has come and gone, you are not my child, as you have shown so in your misdeeds." He held the match in his hand, threw it to his former child and walked away, ignoring the screams of agony and despair as their flesh melted in the unquenched flames until they died. He then went to the one of the ten who had despite all the trials and tests of life had maintained love and adoration for him, had abided by his document of purity and said to his child, "You my child have done all that I have asked and have been faithful to my gracious words. I give you all that I have and more. Come with me to a utopian place that I have been away preparing for you. I love you my child!" The child was made to forget of the existence of her siblings as the memory of their impure deeds and punishment would cause her grief, though she was now in a blissful state in a blissful place. And so it was that the one of ten went with the father and they lived happily ever after in their own paradise, the pure father and child, together, forever...

Some people may see the parable I have written as extreme, but is it? This is the contest, which the gospel lays out in plain terms. It's unflattering, but is the black and white version of what so many believe and accept from their God. The basic gospel of the good news is the part where the father says that he will give you eternal bliss if you follow him. The harder part of the story is the absolute disregard the father has for his own children who were impure and not worthy of him. Would this father be a good father on earth? Would you want him to be your neighbor? Would you like to model your parental ideals after him? These were the questions I had to ask myself when I was ready to face it all with objectivity.

This parable is the Gospel in a nutshell and I accepted it for 27 years. This is the good news that I was so excited about when I was a child. In reality, the statistic of one out of ten people making it to heaven according to the good news of the gospel is still too large of a statistic. This is the reality of the good news if you choose to look at it with an honest eye. I had to think about it and really take the time to imagine my fellow humans, children of God, full of the same love, hate, aspiration and desperation that I felt, doomed to a place of weeping and the gnashing of teeth.

It seemed impossible, but it was always placed in the light of my own innocence and love for God. In my mind I told myself over and over: I love God and want to do his will. I want to please him and show him that I can be good. I will pray to the wind and know he hears me. I will have faith that he hears and I will look for his answers in the subtlest of hints in the world I see and the words of others around me. I will fight the good fight for righteousness!

But the fight went on in my heart and mind. The arguments and justifications continued. I would say to myself: When you are so busy doing good, why would you worry about what would happen if you were bad? This was my mindset and the mindset of so many others. After years of accepting this, it even become a bit of a joke.

Take these lyrics from a Christian music group of my childhood, "The Imperials":

Well, Old Buddha was a man and I'm sure that he meant well
But I pray for his disciples lest they wind up in hell
And I'm sure that old Mohammed thought he knew the way
But it won't be Hare Krishna we stand before on The Judgment Day.

No, it won't be old Buddha that's sitting on the throne
And it won't be old Mohammed that's calling us Home
And it won't be Hare Krishna that plays that trumpet tune
And we're going to see The Son, not Reverend Moon!

Well, I don't hate anybody so please don't take me wrong
But there really is a message to this simple song

You see there's only one-way Jesus if eternal life is your goal
Meditation of the mind won't save your soul.

The Gospel changes lives and inspires people. It makes people want to share it to the world. If God loves you and Jesus loves you so much he died for you, how could that be wrong? Seeing good people who have accepted the good news made me feel strong in my faith, which is why my church was such a powerful place. It united us believers with an understanding of community; after all, these are our brothers and sisters who will be with us in heaven in our perfected state.
Like so many other messages given to us through the annals of history, perspective can really change the meaning of it all. The victor writes the history we read and the perspective of the aggressed is lost. So while the damage done to the unbeliever was awful, I found a way to hide myself in golden, sheltering rays of God's mercy, but it didn't last. Eventually the self-opposing house of cards fell to my common sense and my bullish determination to know and believe real truth gave way to a rejection of what the Gospel message of the Bible as we know it conveys.

BATTLING WITH DEMONS

Be sober-minded; be watchful. Your adversary the devil prowls around like a roaring lion, seeking someone to devour. - 1 Peter 5:8 (NIV)

When I was a child, I often had dreams in which I was very small and my room was very big. In these dreams, a presence lorded over me and gave me the feeling you get when you are about to vomit, but cannot. I heard sounds in the attic of my home of a being yelling and screaming for me, the stompers stomping their feet. In the church of my childhood, all the lights went dark and I was alone in the open space of the gymnasium, being watched all around by unseen forces of evil. I was told that the devil wanted to find and destroy the souls of the young and innocent. He wanted to make them his own and sought to gain access to them in any way he could.

In my years of study, the issue of spiritual warfare, ghosts, demonic activity, aliens and the occult have been my pet area of interest. It is a world behind the veil of what we see and know that I believe really exists. To the Christian mind, virtually anything that is not a directly angelic experience is plainly of the devil. If you see a ghost, it is a demon in disguise. If you see an angel that tells you something that is not the gospel, it is a demon. If you have a nightmare, it is the devil trying to gain access to you. Again, these were very explicit things that I was taught at a very young age. I believed them fully and had fearful experiences to back up the idea that something evil was lurking in the dark, waiting to attack. One of the greatest proofs to the reality that Jesus was the way to salvation was that when I called upon Jesus in the middle of what I saw as a demonic attack, the attack would stop! We referenced what Jesus said in Luke 10:19 (NIV): Behold, I have given you authority to tread on serpents and scorpions, and over all the power of the enemy, and nothing will injure you.

I knew that Jesus was the Son of God who died for my sins and this was a clear way in which I could prove it! Over my 27 years as a Christian, this was one of the clearest ways in which I connected with God, through the fighting of a seemingly demonic experience. There is no greater proof of a truth than a truth that has been experienced on your own. People can say what they want, but when it has been experienced, it takes on a whole new light. But in matters of the spiritual realm, not everything is the way it seems. Just as easily as a person can say that a ghost is a demon in disguise, appearing simply to mislead you into some hellish lie that will draw you from the truth of God, a person could say that a ghost is proof that the story of the Christian afterlife is a falsehood. So which is it? Are these spirits agents of heaven or hell? It all depends on whom you ask.

When I was on my tour to China, there were many Hawaiian kids that were a part of the group. One Hawaiian kid, Brad, spoke about how his uncle was driving along a highway that cut through the center of Oahu. As he drove on, he saw an old woman walking along the side of the road. As he passed she looked at him in his eyes, in a split second. After passing her far enough to nearly be out of her line of sight, he looked in his rear view mirror to see if she was out of sight. Just as he looked into his mirror, he saw her in his back seat and gasped and slammed his brakes and threw his car into park.
He leapt out of the car in terror, only to find that his back seat was empty. In Hawaii, Pele, the mother spirit of the island chain often meets travelers along the road as an old woman, often

angry and instilling fear. According to the folklore of the island, She is not happy with the steel and concrete covering her land and shows up from time to time to express her disdain for people who show too little care for her land. There are innumerable stories of Pele appearing as an old woman, or as a young and beautiful woman, depending on how she felt about the particular person.

In my studies, I have read about people who have felt the call of a spirit for them to become a medicine man. This is an ancient ritual and calling, one that likely predates any other form of religious practice. For this reason, I believe it should not be discounted as drivel. In these stories, there is often a theme of being taken away to a cave, or into the sky and dissected. These would-be medicine men go through terrible torture and dismemberment at the hands of these spirits and are returned to their original state with the ability to heal and predict the future. On one hand, these spirits do evil deeds to these shamanic prospects, but on the other, they give them extraordinary gifts that enrich the lives of the community. So are they evil or good?

I had my own experience just before I decided to become a minister. As I slept, I saw an image of a man covered in red meat musculature, even his face was covered in muscle tissue. This man-like being grabbed right into my stomach and pulled at my intestines, as if to tear them up or out. I woke up with the experience continuing on and I was terrified. I called out to Jesus and the being left me. I couldn't help but wonder if this was some kind of attack to keep me from going to a theology school, but now, in light of learning how a shaman is called, could it be that my hunger to be a spiritual leader was being answered by a shamanic helper, who despite my lack of understanding was attempting to tear me apart as is the tradition among animistic cultures? Was it good, or evil?

In the Amazon and elsewhere around the world, many shamanic healers go into altered states of consciousness through various methods, including rhythmic dance or songs, austerity, or the use of various entheogenic substances. Once in these states, the Amazon and it's plants and animals convey powerful messages to them, instructing them on ways to heal the sick, make medicinal tinctures and intervene against evil spirits. Once again, these spiritual beings are sometimes even the spirits of, or behind these plants. Why would evil spirits want to intervene with the lives of simple people and give them medicines that work to heal the sick? The idea that all of these spirits that people experience all over the world are all demons from the pit of hell simply does not make sense.

The Bible clearly speaks against trying to commune with the dead for any purpose. In fact, this practice is directly connected to witchcraft. The raising of the spirits of the long dead was not possible, because we go to either heaven or hell's waiting room. There is no middle ground for the spirits of men to abide on the earth. Hebrews 9:27 (NIV) says:
And inasmuch as it is appointed for men to die once and after this comes judgment.

So, a man's soul cannot be roaming the earth according to the New Testament, but what does the Old Testament have to say on the matter? Surely, there must be continuity since the Bible is the inerrant word of God, correct? Let's see what is said in 1 Samuel 28:8-18 (NIV):

Then Saul disguised himself by putting on other clothes, and went, he and two men with him, and they came to the woman by night; and he said, "Conjure up for me, please, and bring up for me whom I shall name to you. But the woman said to him, "Behold, you know what Saul has done, how he has cut off those who are mediums and spiritists from the land. Why are you then laying a snare for my life to bring about my death? Saul vowed to her by the LORD, saying, "As the LORD lives, no punishment shall come upon you for this thing. Then the woman said, "Whom shall I bring up for you?" And he said, "Bring up Samuel for me. When the woman saw Samuel, she cried out with a loud voice; and the woman spoke to Saul, saying, "Why have you deceived me? For you are Saul! The king said to her, "Do not be afraid; but what do you see?" And the woman said to Saul, "I see a divine being coming up out of the earth. He said to her, "What is his form?" And she said, "An old man is coming up, and he is wrapped with a robe." And Saul knew that it was Samuel, and he bowed with his face to the ground and did homage. Then Samuel said to Saul, "Why have you disturbed me by bringing me up?"

In this passage we see a Hebrew king pulling up a dead familiar spirit through a witch! So, what is the station of the witch? Does she pull up a holy soul like that of the prophet Samuel by the power of the Devil? Which is it? Is the spirit by which the witch works that of good or evil? She is breaking Mosaic Law in the body of this text and yet is fully capable of drawing up a spirit. I bring this up because it begs the question, what are these spirits? Are they the ghosts of the dead, or demons trying to fool us? In the text we just read, it was of a holy prophet. Looking at this from an outside perspective, something does not jive; it's as if there is a double standard being laid out. As we read in the book of Hebrews, souls go straight to heaven, into the hands of God, but in 1 Samuel even witches can pull them from the hands of God! This is just one example of how we get a mixed message about what happens to you after you die. It also gives us a mixed message about who the evil spirits are, who are the appropriate people to consult on matters of spirituality and what can be done to, or with your soul after you are dead.

Time after time, I came back to the foundational authority of Jesus over evil spirits. He has given us authority over, "serpents and scorpions" and therefore made us capable of shooing away evil spirits. In Ephesians 6:12 (NIV), it says: "For our struggle is not against flesh and blood, but against the rulers, against the powers, against the world forces of this darkness, against the spiritual forces of wickedness in the heavenly places."
So, if we take the Bible as the source of true information, we know that there are unseen

rulers and powers that abide in heavenly places. Apparently, we wrestle with these beings, but as Christians, we have the power to squelch them. If you have ever stumbled upon a faith healer on television, you might have seen a WWF wrestling style event in which demons are cast out of people and others are healed. Today, we can see a slick-haired man in an expensive suit cast out demons in the name of Jesus. We can call demons away from ourselves by simply the power of his name. So this is proof that Jesus is who he said he was, the Son of God who has come to save our souls, right? Well, no. Every faith has healers like these and Christians simply tell you that any non-Christian healer is using the power of the devil, but if that is the case, by what power did the witch of Endor, whom Saul consulted, conjure up Samuel? The answer is unclear. What is clear is the fact that there are spirits all around us, some good, and some evil. But a solid way of knowing exactly what, or who they are, is simply a matter of personal opinion.

I for so long asked myself why there is an overwhelmingly large amount of negative spiritual occurrences in the Christian faith? Why does demonic activity pervade the landscape? Should it not be that people are constantly encountering positive angelic beings and God himself? This has never been the case for me and seems to not have been the case for the many Christians I have known in my life. To me, the negative supernatural activity seems to fit quite nicely with the fear based ideas of a hellish afterlife and the idea that we need Christ as a constant shield against this evil onslaught. It's like mystic mafia protection as long as you stay in line with the mafia's demands!

So what do we do if these beings are real? What do the non-Christians do to keep themselves from the influence and attacks of these malevolent beings from beyond? Once again, it depends on whom you ask. Much of it depends on your state of mind and how you feel about yourself. My personal thought is that Jesus was stating something that was true for all time before him. We all have the authority over our own souls and therefore are fully capable of telling evil things to leave us alone. We are children of the light, whose eternal souls are precious treasures among all the wonders of the universe. I have experienced this first hand. Upon some sort of dream or feeling in which I felt there was a spiritual attack, I would simply let the being know it had no authority over me, because I was a child of God.

For the Christian reader, you may be scratching your head, wondering how I can believe in God, but not Christianity. Well, the truth is, I've discovered that Christianity is a latecomer in the contest of who and what God is. Long before Christ, Osiris was wrongfully killed and resurrected to become the lord of the afterlife. In Hindu thought, God is consciousness and we exist as an extension of him/her. This is the idea that we are God and God is us. One may wrongly misunderstand that someone believing this thinks that they are God. This is not the case. People who believe this simply understand that the love and life we experience and are a part of is of God and is the physical manifestation of God in us. Just like cells are in your body, but are not your body as a whole, so we are with God. And if every cell in our body resonates with God and his consciousness, then we have always had God as close to us as possible. In the scenario of the Shamanic initiate, they undergo a desert period just like Jesus and suffer a horrible fate, only to return victorious over the forces of evil. The theme of dying and returning to destroy evil is not exclusive to any one faith.

Ultimately, it doesn't matter how you view God in matters of the spiritual realm. You may be poked, prodded and harassed by what you perceive to be evil, but you have authority over your soul. It is a gift from God that cannot be taken away by anyone or anything. Living with this understanding gives you the boldness to defend yourself. You don't have to have a heavy knowledge of the universe's greatest mysteries for it to be so.

But, some may still wonder why the name of Jesus causes demons to flee?
In the same way that a salvation experience changes your heart and mind, so does the name of Jesus equip you with a feeling of authority. The authority over evil has always been there, but the name of Jesus gives you the confidence when you did not have it before. It's like putting a cape on a child; they become a superhero! Jesus is the cape that makes you feel like a spiritual superhero. It's as simple as that.
Equipped with this understanding, we don't have to live in fear that we are somehow outside of the grace and protection of God, because God is bigger than the story of the Bible and is a part of you right now. There is no need to live in fear of the unknown. You will be perfectly safe.
In the world of spirits, demons, ghosts and other unknown beings, there is much to be learned. If we stop living in fear, we take away the greatest weapon any spiritual adversary has against us.

We are able to grasp a brighter light and feel the love of those who have passed away. They do come to visit us from time to time; so don't be religiously offended by your dead grandma when she pays you a ghostly visit!

If I have done my job of explanation well, you should now feel equipped to see the spiritual world as a wonderful place that can be explored. It is true that there are evil spirits, but there are bad people too. I have realized in my post-Christian experiences that the existence of bad people in the world doesn't make me feel the need to stay inside for my whole life. No, I get up and go about my business, and learn, love and thrive. In the same way, I don't feel afraid of the spiritual world just because there are bad spirits, that's just as silly as locking myself up at home in the physical realm. The sun is shining and the birds are singing outside and so it is beyond the veil of our perception. To miss the splendor available to us in the spiritual realms is as sad as missing a walk in the park on a sunny day. My experiences have taught me to go forth with confidence and that I am sovereign over myself in the physical and the spiritual worlds.

WOLVES AMONG THE SHEEP

I don't want to talk about this, but I feel it must be plainly confronted.

The authority system of Christianity makes it a hornet's nest for evil. The vilest of practices and activities are performed behind closed doors and so many young people's lives are forever marred by molestation and rape at the hands of pastors, priests and other spiritual leaders.

As I write this now, one of the most prominent mega-church pastors in America is getting a divorce, having had several men come forward with allegations that he had sodomized them as their "spiritual father".

According to the allegations, he would take up a father role with these misguided youth and would bring them encouragement and support. They would go on trips together to strengthen their "spiritual bond". After some time had passed and these young men were in a place of financial support from him, he would then coerce them into consummation of their deep bond, through oral and anal sex

But how big of a problem is this really? The issue was pretty well characterized when the April, 2008 edition of Christianity Today said this:

In the last three years, an average of 23 new articles each day have appeared in secular media sources revealing sexual abuse allegations arising in Protestant churches in the United States. Protestant denominations have been tempted to call sexual abuse a "Catholic problem"; this is simply not true. Within the past eight years, verdicts, judgments, or settlements exceeding hundreds of millions of dollars have been levied against Protestant churches for sexual abuse allegations arising from children participating in ministry programs.

The church and its children are increasingly endangered by sexual predators whose opportunity to ensnare children elsewhere is growing smaller, while the church opens its doors to anyone. Sexual abusers looking for access to children will gravitate to activities and organizations where there are fewer protective measures in place. Secular organizations have responded to this inevitable truth by implementing policies and training to reduce risk. Many churches, however, have done little, because ministries fail to recognize the risks or are laboring under the misconception "it won't happen here."

The rape and molestation of children is a real problem in the Protestant and Catholic churches. The problem is so widespread that churches now frequently take insurance against lawsuits that may come from molestations.
This problem is close to my heart, as I am the father of two small children who attend churches regularly. Because they live with their mother, I have no idea who they are exposed to. I am not convinced by comments like, "He's a really great guy! He's really supportive of the kids!" I am not comforted or convinced by statements like this because this problem is very close to home for me.

John was the principal at my Lutheran Private School during my jr. high years. He was a handsome and inspirational man with a decade of excellent results in educating children. He was also a manly man who played sports and coached our basketball team. In the jr. high years, a boy begins his journey to manhood and thirsts for guidance and examples of how to be a man. I was no different in this regard. All of us hung upon John's words as he led our basketball team to a league victory. Kids at this age don't always know what boundaries are appropriate with adults and there were certainly times in which those boundaries were crossed with us.

When at leisure time, someone was always giving him a back massage or sitting in his lap. I did this as well and didn't think it was weird at the time. Now it completely creeps me out to think back on it. He always seemed to have a favorite kid that he would provide more praise and adoration for in our school events. There was always a punishment and reward system in place that kept us in line. If we were good, we were allowed to go on special trips or field days. If we were bad, we were not allowed to go to recess, or special trips. Our progress was tallied on a chart that everyone could see in order to embarrass the bad and lavish praise upon the good.

When children were especially bad, they would be spanked, using "Elsie", the paddle used for corporal punishment. He would say at the beginning of each school term, "behave yourself, or Elsie!" while waiving his paddle in the air. Everyone spanked by him had to write his or her name on the paddle. It was covered in tiny signatures. To many in the Christian community, spanking children past the age of 12 is totally acceptable. In fact, a recent youtube.com video shows South Texas judge, William Adams, "Disciplining" his 16-year-old daughter for using the Internet. How this behavior is acceptable in this day and age is one of the most disgusting and scary aspects of the American-Christian culture.

At the end of every school year, John would take a handful of us "good kids" to Moclipse, WA as a reward. We would go ride go-carts and play on the beach. We would play games and had trust activities that we were all to participate in, like the falling into each other's arms as we fell backward. When it was time for sleep, all of us would sleep in the living room area of condo in which we were staying. John's favorite kid would sleep in his bed with him. I don't know that anything bad happened on that trip, but I don't know how that kid's parents would have felt had they known that a grown man had recommended that he sleep in his bed with him. I certainly would not!

In my freshman year of high school, it was discovered that John had been accused of indecent liberties with a young man from a few years back. The story was very similar to the mega-church pastor at the beginning of this chapter. John would favor this boy and make him feel good. He would encourage and take more time with him to help him in his studies. The Morning News Tribune posted this article on April 4th, 1992:

LUTHERAN PRINCIPAL ACCUSED. Denying charges of indecent liberties with a student is John-----, who resigned in March as principal of Central Lutheran Christian School, Tacoma. Now a senior, the youth said ------- took him on outings and French kissed him for hours when he was a 5th grader, and tried to masturbate him at a state park after plying him with whiskey. A teenager said, "He had kids at his house a lot." John was convicted and spent a few years in a Federal prison and is now a registered sex-offender.

Now I was in high school and certainly out of the woods of creepy Christian child molesters, right? Not quite. I spoke earlier about Herman in chapter 1. Herman was the youth group pastor of my church and was an electrifying character. He was a talented singer and sharp-witted individual who had the support of our prominent and popular mega-church pastor, Bill. Herman would often schedule trips for the youth group to attend. We had a winter camp and a summer camp and various other trips organized every year. Teens would often go to Herman's house upon invitation for Bible studies or prayer meetings. I had been to his house once for some spiritual advice, which he gave without incident.

During my experiences with him, I always looked up to him as a great spiritual leader and example of what a godly man could be. He always provided solid biblical teaching with a modern and easily digestible feel. There was no perceived reason to ever think anything about him other than how cool he was! After church, many kids would go to the local restaurant and eat. When kids didn't have money, he would pay for their meals. He did this for me on a few occasions. A few years after I graduated from high school, The Seattle Times posted an article on June 5th, 1999:

TACOMA - Another teen came forward yesterday to allege he was sexually molested by a (church) youth pastor, according to Pierce County sheriff's spokesman Ed Troyer. Meanwhile, elders from the church defended their handling of a 1995 complaint against the youth pastor now charged with eight counts of child molestation and rape, saying the 4-year-old allegations against (Herman) amounted to "hearsay." The elders also said in a statement that (Herman) was returned to his job only after they were assured he would not be a threat to children.

Prosecutors on Thursday charged (Herman), 34, with eight counts stemming from alleged assaults on two teenage boys beginning last year. Possible cases involving as many as 16 other boys here and in the Chicago area remained under investigation. Troyer said the teen who came forward yesterday would be interviewed by detectives and the prosecutor's office.

(Herman) resigned his post at the 2,000-member church Tuesday, citing "gross moral failures by engaging in sexual contact with minors." He was being held on $75,000 bail in Pierce County Jail on six counts of third-degree rape, one count of second-degree rape and one count of child molestation. He has pleaded not guilty.

The boys described a grooming process that involved passwords and progressive levels of contact between them and (Herman), prosecutors said. (he) reportedly told authorities he would pretend to be sleepwalking or talking in his sleep to get the boys to engage in sex acts. "A lot of mind control was involved in it," Troyer said.

No sexual contact involving the two boys occurred at the church, but it did at (his) home in University Place, charging papers said.

(Herman) said church officials had no knowledge of what he'd done before his admission. In their statement, the council of elders said (Herman) came to the Tacoma church in 1991 with "glowing recommendations"....

So what's the point of bringing this up? It is unreasonable to think that every church is full of people looking to sexually abuse our children, right? My personal experiences with this grave subject, coupled with the statistics show that the church is an unchecked place that is ripe for child-molesters and rapists posing to be very normal and even inspirational characters. With so many fine and upstanding people who attend churches and earnestly try to enrich the lives of others, it's so hard to discern wolves from the sheep, especially when we are dealing with a scenario that allows plenty of room for sinister individuals with "glowing recommendations" to do their work.

Of course we know this is a reality that is obviously not exclusive to protestant clergy. We all have heard countless stories about the catholic molestations and their cover-ups. It cannot be ignored or talked away and should be a warning to those who think that their church leaders are somehow different from those in other churches.

There is a double standard that comes with this subject. On one hand, most Christian denominations firmly believe homosexuality to be a sin and will not allow homosexuals to participate in ministry. On the other hand, Christian leaders are sodomizing and molesting our children. I believe that the basic doctrines of Christianity help to cause this problem. When you have people who are closet homosexuals, but must hide it for fear of being rejected by God and ministers, they have a build up of sexual tension.

The only way to release that tension is to perform homosexual acts in a way that nobody else will find out. If sneaking off to gay bars and other places is too difficult because of prominence in the ministry, then it would seem that the easiest way to compensate is to lure and abuse children. This is a problem that doesn't have a solution. So as long as this double standard prevails, there will be continued cases of sexual abuse, rape and molestation. In my opinion, its enough to not want to set foot in a church again with my children.

I am in no way saying that homosexuals in general have any sort of disposition towards children, because that is absolutely untrue. Ironically, the stigma of child molestation, especially of men of the church over boys adds to the doctrinal stance that homosexuals in general seek relations with children. The schism caused by judgmental behavior and the association of homosexuals with sex offenders is simply inaccurate, unacceptable and saddening to me. I take these events seriously and am so grateful that these monsters that were literally in my inner circle of trust did not hurt me. I feel so sad for the victims of these people and their misdeeds.

It would be much easier to just bury our heads in the sand and pretend like the problem doesn't exist, but while good people try to live good lives, churches and clergies try to hide these evil deeds and cover them up in any way they can. Where is the light and holiness? Again, just like in the world of spirits, we seem find the demons more than the angels in Christianity.

US VS. THEM

In the beginning scenes of the movie, "Red Dawn", Russian paratroopers are seen falling from the sky and into the baseball field of a rural high school. The kids all freak out and start making their way for the hills. They end up fighting for freedom from the Communist invaders!

I grew up in the 80's, where such polarizing and frightening sights, sounds and propaganda taught me that Russians were bad and America was good. When I went to church, I learned that the Devil was bad and that God was good. When I went to school, I learned that other religions were bad and that Christianity was good. Everywhere I looked, I was given black and white answers for a black and white world. I didn't need to wonder if I was in a moral grey area, I had the bible to tell me unequivocally what needed to be done and what needed to be avoided.

Life was so easy and carefree, when I knew whom my enemies were. This made it easy for me to know which political views were appropriate. I supported Republicans because they were mostly Christian. Ronald Reagan was the greatest president ever and George Bush Sr. was pretty good too. The people on the other side of politics were godless, baby aborting sodomites who craved depravity and communism. They wanted to take away our guns put drugs in the hands of our children; their bleeding hearts were a farce. Their leaders were sleazy scumbags who were more interested in meeting hookers in secret hotels rather than doing any good for our great country.

Was this just my mindset built from my familial surroundings, or was there something more to it? In my studies, I've found that I had been prepped and conditioned, not just by my American culture, but also by the Bible itself. I realized that the "us vs. them" theme even allowed room for genocide in the name of God. 1 Samuel 15:2-3 says:

This is what the LORD Almighty says: 'I will punish the Amalekites for what they did to Israel when they waylaid them as they came up from Egypt. Now go, attack the Amalekites and totally destroy everything that belongs to them. Do not spare them; put to death men and women, children and infants, cattle and sheep, camels and donkeys.

I thought at first that maybe this was just a misunderstanding? Clearly, it was not. Once again I saw a mandate for permissible genocide in Deuteronomy 20:16-18:

Only in the cities of these peoples that the LORD your God is giving you as an inheritance, you shall not leave alive anything that breathes. "But you shall utterly destroy them, the Hittite and the Amorite, the Canaanite and the Perizzite, the Hivite and the Jebusite, as the LORD your God has commanded you, so that they may not teach you to do according to all their detestable things which they have done for their gods, so that you would sin against the LORD your God.

How was I supposed to reconcile this? Many Christians claimed that this mass genocide of untold thousands of people; men, women, children, infants and livestock was in response to the fact that these groups worshipped Gods other than Jehovah. Many of these groups of people belonged to ancient sex cults and performed rites in which they sacrificed their children to their god, Molech. In my young mind, I somehow allowed myself to accept this as a reasonable excuse for such clearly abhorrent behavior.

My conscience kept asking: was the sin of these people really a valid reason for genocide though? The donkeys were not performing these practices that Jehovah didn't approve of. There is once again a moral turn I had to take; either I would have to accept that genocide is ok if the God of the Bible says it's ok, or the God of the Bible is a blood soaked maniac. In my devotion to God, I figured that he was greater than me and ultimately was righteous in any deed he wanted his people to perform. Even Jesus showed that there is a time for "us vs. them" partiality when he was harassed by a Canaanite woman in Matthew 15:21-28 (NIV):

Jesus left that place and went away to the district of Tyre and Sidon. Just then a Canaanite woman from that region came out and started shouting, 'Have mercy on me, Lord, Son of David; my daughter is tormented by a demon.' But he did not answer her at all. And his disciples came and urged him, saying, 'Send her away, for she keeps shouting after us.' He answered, 'I was sent only to the lost sheep of the house of Israel.' But she came and knelt before him, saying, 'Lord, help me.' He answered, 'It is not fair to take the children's food and throw it to the dogs.' She said, 'Yes, Lord, yet even the dogs eat the crumbs that fall from their masters' table.' Then Jesus answered her, 'Woman, great is your faith! Let it be done for you as you wish.' And her daughter was healed instantly.

In this passage, I saw Jesus calling a Canaanite woman a dog while referring to his people as children. Only because of her persistence does he help her. Biblical examples like these justified my worldview. The bottom line was that God's people were in the right and God's holy justice could be dealt through the hands of his servants. When I accepted these fringy concepts from the Bible, I would in arguments now say with passion and confidence: These people deserved the wrath they received just like we all do when we decide not to accept God.

Unfortunately, most people conditioned by the "us vs. them" mentality still look at the world in this way today. After 9/11, George Bush Jr. said: If you're not with us, you're against us.

When I saw what had happened on that terrible day and heard the president, I was nearly frothing at the mouth, wanting holy vengeance! I had learned from the Bible that there is a necessary time for relentless, vicious violence and now was that time. Was my critical mind thinking then? Unfortunately not, I was a mental pawn that accepted whatever mandate was sent down to me from my figures of authority. My "us vs. them" triggers clouded my thoughts and turned my sadness for the dead of 9/11 into rage toward our enemies who perpetrated this horrible act of violence.

As a Christian, there was no choice but to accept that there is the "us" side and the "them" side. It's a great template if you think about it, I mean you can plop yourself into the "us" team and only have to find one sinful thing the other side is doing to justify making them "them"! Brilliant! It's true and we do it all of the time. Just like when we used joked amongst ourselves in college about people going to hell and made light of the "lost", we giggled to ourselves while other nations crumbled to ruins under our campaigns of "shock and awe". Of course, we know that the reports we get rarely show us the bodies of women and children who are killed and maimed, or even of our own dead soldiers who died for our country, fulfilling the will of our commander in chief.

This "us vs. them" mentality that I personally subscribed to for so long kept my world in black and white terms and bred contempt for those on the outside. Adhering to the teachings of the Apostle Paul in the New Testament, Christians believe homosexuality is a sin and think that allowing gay marriage will justify the sin of homosexuality in the eyes of the government. This legalization will allow "them" to be normal. Mothers would have to tell their children about how some people love the same sex and get married. But as good Christians, mothers can't bring themselves to call gay love real love, so they would have to say that gays want to make marriage their own because they want to flaunt shamelessness everywhere they choose to go. Christians have to say things suggestively, like, "I think that kind of behavior is icky!" stepping gingerly around the possibility of sounding like a bigot. The "us vs. them" mentality leads and guides us all the way through and justifies our partiality in matters like this. Unfortunately, we are taught this behavior from the same source that we learn of grace and compassion.

Once again, I had to deal with an uncomfortable issue, accept or reject the genocide, accept or reject the idea of hell and accept or reject the homosexuals. If I believed the Bible to be the inerrant word of God, then I had to play the "us vs. them" game. It's simply impossible to avoid.

There are too many subjects like this in which a line is drawn in the sand.

When people with beating hearts and a need for love and kindness just like us are called, "them" in our minds, they no longer hold quite the same value to us. In our presumed innocent minds, they are less than us because, by their lifestyle, faith, or sexual preference they are against the teachings of the Bible. When I grasped this, I realized suddenly how sanctimonious and unwittingly unloving I had become, just like my father in heaven, too pure for "them".

I know this is true, because it was my mindset as a Christian. I was guilty of living in this mentality and am ashamed that I did. It was pounded into my little mind as soon as I could form thoughts. Sure, we had a general compassion for the "lost" and wanted to see people get saved. As I wrote earlier, it was my utmost conviction so save as many souls as I could. It was why I wanted to become a missionary; it was my reason for living. This deep seeded struggle forced me to teeter on the fence about the real nature of my God and I hoped, to my chagrin that other passages in New Testament would be less staunch about the "us vs. them" ideology. Unfortunately, I was set up for disappointment. In Matthew 25:31-33 (NIV) it says:

When the Son of Man comes in his glory, and all the angels with him, he will sit on his glorious throne. All the nations will be gathered before him, and he will separate the people one from another as a shepherd separates the sheep from the goats. He will put the sheep on his right and the goats on his left.

I tried my best to objectively observe passages like this and took note that the good people were sheep; fluffy and adorable, never to harm anyone. On the other had, the bad people were the goats, horned and rough. So again, the "us vs. them" mentality continued on as a strong and subtle theme. Sadly, it is a theme that runs through the Bible from start to finish. You must accept the "us vs. them" mentality in order to get through almost any bit of doctrine in the Bible.

The only argument I could pose now was to ask why it was such a bad thing. I mean there were good and bad people, so why not classify them this way? The biggest danger that this mentality posed to humanity is the propagation of the idea that we are separate. It is my belief that people in general want to live a life of love and happiness. They want to live a life where they are treated fairly and as equals. When we put people into these separating boxes, we end up degrading them, as I have explained. Secondly, the people who control our governments and corporations know that most of us think this way. They love the fact that you think this way. It makes you easy to control. For example, have you ever seen an ad where somebody has a cleaning product that just doesn't work? The lady looks sad and disheveled, maybe a little sleepy. The announcer comes on:

Tired of scrubbing that grime out with inferior products? Don't you wish there was another way to clean better, faster? Well my friends you're in luck, because new Shiny-Brite brand scrubbing stuff cuts your cleanup time in half!

Of course, while the announcer is speaking, they show a new lady who is more attractive than the first and very happy, well kept and relieved to almost be done cleaning. They have just used your "us vs. them" conditioning to tell you what to buy. There are a million examples of this mentality. All you need to do is pay attention to a few commercials to see it at work. When our governments need to go to war again, they tell us about what "they" are doing: They are planning to nuke U.S. cities and we must stop them! We have discovered what they are up to! They want to kill us! Send the troops!

I used to sit on my couch and root for our team, eating the propaganda up. It's not exclusive to any party lines either, this mentality allowed our current president to bomb Libya and for the most part, nobody really complained. While we accept that our government is defending "us", the "them" people of the world wake up to cluster bombs and death.

I've come to realize that this mentality is extremely dangerous. It keeps us separated when we should be unified. It makes us enemies, when we should be friends. Every "them" on this planet has a soul; a father, a mother, children and other loved ones. Every "them" that I laughed about bombing or righteously preached about destroying has all the potential that we now have. We do not live in a black and white world. We are not told the whole story when things happen on a world stage. We are told what has been carefully crafted for us. It is a method that has been perfected over time by people in perpetual states of power. Over time and with much embarrassment over my past mistakes, I have seen another way, to catch myself in my daily life when I begin to think in these terms and stop it. If you try it for a day or two, you will be astonished at just how much this method is used on you in every aspect of your life.

Of course, my opinions are my own and if you are entrenched in your "us vs. them" mentality, you might get angry and call me a heretical backslider. My goal is not to upset anyone, but to help others see what I have discovered to be true, that I had been mentally conditioned by my Christian faith to accept whatever authority is over me and do as I am instructed. I am no different from you. I want to be my own man and make my own decisions, but I don't want to hate, or look down on "them". I don't want there to be a "them" anymore. It's a daily struggle to not fall back into that mentality when disagreements arise, or people cause harm to others. But if we allow our love to lead us, we can fight the temptation to see the world in such degrading terms.

We all want the same things: love, compassion, a belly full of hot food, friendship and protection from harm. The sooner we start to see that "them" are the same as "us", the sooner we can all see these basic human needs fulfilled. If every country we planned to bomb were full of our brothers and sisters, would we bomb them then? If we realized that these other races of people were fellow children of God, would we really think it ever to be acceptable to commit acts of war? Would we look at the deeds of the God of the Bible and perhaps reconsider what kind of God he really was? These are personal matters and decisions I cannot make for anyone else, but I reflect upon these things often and feel that I was misled into believing the "us vs. them" mindset.

When I stepped out of the "us vs. them" mentality, I found myself looking at the world through a whole new set of eyes. Everything that I thought to be true needed to be reconsidered. The way I treated the people I disliked changed. My belief in the core goodness of mankind has changed. There is really no telling where else freedom from this trained mentality will take us, because the change that happens is so big that it can take you in almost any direction. In my experience, that direction is normally a very constructive and positive one.

EXODUS

It is a counterfeit love that is contingent upon authority, punishment, or reward. True love is respect and admiration, compassion and kindness, freely given by a healthy, unafraid human being. – Dan Barker

It was one of the greatest moments of my life when my first child, Gideon was born. It was the first time I realized what it might feel like to be God in the eyes of another. I did not consider myself to be God by any stretch of the imagination, but I did see the parallel that the Bible often draws between a father and his children. This was what I had been waiting for all of my life; the chance to share everything that I had learned and pass it on. As I looked into his crib just moments after he was born, I made a solemn promise to him: I will never withhold the truth from you. I will always do my best to protect you from harm. I will love you no matter what or whom you choose to become. You will always be my son and I will always be your father.

I spoke these words without terms or conditions. They are as eternal as my living soul and shall remain unchanged. When I spoke these words, something changed within me. The seeds of doubt began to take seed, not in my love for my son, but in my belief that the God I had devoted my life to in ministry did not say the same thing to me as I did to my son.

This made me wonder how it could be that I, being a sinful human father could make an unconditional promise, but the non-human and perfect God of the Bible could not. At this time, I was 23 years old and my faith was very deeply planted in me. As the years passed, this feeling that something was wrong never left me, but slowly eroded the pillars of my faith like a river carves through stone.

The best way for me to compensate for this was to take even greater leaps of faith in my daily life. I moved across country again and started a new Christian band to minister full time with. I prayed hard and joined a dynamic church in Seattle with a kind-hearted pastor. I fought and prayed against my vice of viewing pornography, thinking that this regular sin was the key thing eroding my faith from within. I did everything that I could to keep myself in a positive state of mind.

In the meantime, my beautiful daughter Gwyneth was born. I made my fatherly promise once again. By this time, I was knee deep in touring with my band and trying to raise a family. It's hard enough to attempt to do this well when you are stable and not traveling all over. It's extremely taxing when you cannot make decisions for your own family because you must consider the needs of the other families involved in your group. It was at this point that I decided that the band ministry idea was not sustainable with a wife and two children. I then chose to resign from the group and return to college to finish my degree.

I felt like this was a great way to restore my faith and get on a path that would bring my small family together in a way that we all could participate. I found myself trying to decide how I would revitalize my faith and remembered my inspiring times in YWAM.

As I stated before, the Kings Kids program was sponsored by a Christian missionary agency known as Youth With A Mission. At the time of my participation, good family friends, Tom and Cindy were the leaders. They had moved on to a new missionary venture that focused primarily on using surfing as a method of outreach to otherwise unapproachable groups of people. This idea sounded fantastic to me because I loved surfing and loved the idea of reuniting with Tom and Cindy. They were and still are the finest examples of the best kind of traditional Christian possible. Even through all of this excitement, I had been suppressing my doubt in Christianity for some time and it was beginning to fester.

When in college, I saw the strange Pentecostal revival behaviors that were prized and the strange way that people spoke about the lost. It was a sort of pity mixed with disdain and a light glaze of real compassion. I was also beginning to see that the world had more to offer than just Christianity. There were a whole host of ideas and thoughts that were shared in local newspapers and magazines that seemed to make sense to me, but should not have because of my beliefs in the Bible.

Somehow without any outside source pulling me, my festering doubt met with outside wisdom that made more sense than what I believed as a Christian. I started to realize that I was in a small mental world of my own creation. I had somehow been conditioned to see the world one way and one way alone, through the filter of the

Bible. My heart wanted so bad to please God, but my mind kept showing me things that didn't make sense. I would talk to people who had a strong understanding of the world and provided me with perspectives that I had never been able to grasp previously. I was now awakening rapidly and the schism between my wife and myself was widening.

By the time my first quarter of my final school year was complete, I was not a believer. I only say this in retrospect because it's the reality I refused to believe at the time. I couldn't even share my doubts with anyone in the school or the ministry because they would not allow me to graduate if this were the case. This period of time was the dusk that led to the dark year and was mingled with much confusion and numbed pain. I felt like I had left the world of music, the only thing I could be good at to build a family and try to find something else to make my frantically creative mind satisfied. I tried to gain financial backing for my missionary plans, but none would come to fruition. I tried to dig deeper into the Greek texts of the New Testament and only found more complications to my already mounting troubles with my faith.

One morning in school, a teacher relayed to us

the way that you can spot a cult. In Christian circles, cults are groups that claim to be Christian, but do not adhere to the doctrines set out by the Ante-Nicene creed. We were told stories about many people who were riddled with guilt and harassed by cult members and even threatened in various manners. It was all very shocking and scary to consider that this sort of thing was going on! The teacher laid out the descriptors of a cult;

-A cult will welcome you at first, asking nothing of you, but will often give you things you essentially have a need for. Food and shelter are often provided.
-A cult will tell you that their version of the truth is the only way and that only their leader is the true person to get you to heaven
-A cult will pressure you to give them money in increasing amounts and will find ways to make you feel the absolute need to give money to them.
-A cult will threaten you that if you attempt to leave the group, your soul will be eternally punished.
-If you leave the cult, the members will turn their backs on you and will take every opportunity to slander your name and reputation.

When I heard the descriptions listed, I realized

117

that the Christians around me behaved exactly in this way! At the time of this transition in my life, I lived in tremendous fear that I was going to burn in hell even for having doubt in my faith. In retrospect, the above description of a cult could quite easily be the condensed version of how I was treated when I outwardly rejected Christianity; I was threatened, harassed, blacklisted and exiled. The Church itself was a Cult! In historical records, early Christians were often referred to as a cult of Judaism. Even today, many Jews view Christianity in this manner.

Now that I knew that I was a part of a cult and that the God I worshipped sent his own children to hell and the outside world made a lot more sense on many basic issues. It was this triple realization that was simply too much to bear. By the time this realization was fully in place, the rift between who I was becoming and who my wife continued to be was too vast and I knew it. In many ways, I could see it coming for years in all the ways I didn't want to see it, but it was there all along, creeping in the corners of my mind. Now I understood the Biblical love of God to be a counterfeit and I felt a similar love lost in my relationship towards my wife. We had built our relationship on the foundation of

Christianity and without that foundation, there was very little that we ended up having in common. I had so much love for my children and so many worries and troubles in my mind:

If I am not a Christian, who am I then?

If I leave the Church and my wife, what will happen next?

I knew from a lifetime of experience with Christians what the outcome would be and what their answers were. I wasn't stupid; I could have lip-synched the answers as they said them. The problem was not that I had somehow lost my way within my faith and relationships; it was that I knew the answers within the parameters of my faith were simply no longer sufficient to help.

These feelings I had and the dark year that was to come are the reason that I am writing this book. In a state like this, you feel like you have nowhere to run and hide, no one to turn to who can somehow make you feel like it's going to be ok. You are under the microscope of everyone you know. And you must be surer of this than anything else, for who can save you from the wrath of God if you are wrong? Who will be your friend if all of your friends are Christians?

Who is really leftover when the you that you have built in your faith is no more? It is a harrowing experience which tests and tempers a man. Like water going down a drain, I swirled into the center of the vortex, to be shot through a pipeline of confusion. My former shepherd no longer led me beside the still waters of Psalm 23.

With so much doubt and a sense that what I had believed was not the truth, I looked outside of my faith at what might as well have been a black hole. But with no choice in my mind, but to make drastic changes in my search for truth in my life, I had to take the plunge. The steps I took were like the steps of a drunken blind man, though, for it was not anything I was familiar with. As I stepped into the dark, I only knew one alternative to trying to be a good Christian; to become the beast.

THE DARK YEAR

He who makes a beast of himself gets rid of the pain of being a man – Hunter S. Thompson

I was 21 years old when I married my 19-year-old college sweetheart. We spent most of our time trying to find ways to serve God and make a living doing so. For nearly 7 years we lived in low-income situations for the sake the gospel that we devoted our lives to. When I no longer believed the gospel, my dissatisfaction spilled over into the rest of my thoughts and behaviors. I became restless and unexcited about anything remotely Christian and that was all that I was surrounded by. At night, I would go out to a new world that was so foreign and beguiling to me; a world I used to call sinful, but now was not so sure. The only way to really know was to go and be a part of it. Several months before I moved out of the apartment, I told my wife that I didn't want to be in the marriage with her. She being very passive, had little to say or do beyond that except to suggest that we visit a Christian counselor. I refused, knowing that more

Christian half-light and advice was what I was trying to get away from. This state put our relationship in a stalemate that awkwardly lasted for many months. By the time I graduated, I was ready to leave.

I moved 15 minutes away from my kids and began working security at a nightclub. I started dating a girl fresh out of rehab and at first lived with her as she worked on her sobriety. I somehow viewed this as a way for my girlfriend and I to find a common ground in our own rebirth as new people. Around this time, I also reunited with my best childhood friend, Big Man. He had been down a very different road than I had traveled thus far and was in many ways a great comfort for my troubled mind. We started to spend a lot more time together while I began investing more energy into going to clubs and bars in the hip area of Seattle. Big Man and I would go out and drink and make merry, something I had not ever really done with any sort of regularity. In a way, it was what I should have been doing in my early 20's and not as I approached the end of them. Since I was so strongly excited about starting over, I poured all the same passion I had into my friendships and relationships without them fully being vetted for the amount that I would give. My girlfriend at the time relapsed and I followed her into the void, learning the ways of the drug culture. Throughout this period, I would have realizations that our relationship was very vitriolic and would leave her, only for her to try to find ways back in my life. When I was not dating her, I dated other girls who were trouble, girls who were as far from my former faith as possible. I was a pendulum in full swing; I was good and now, I would be evil. Evil has a way of taking you further than you want to go, longer than you want to stay, telling you more than you're willing to know and charging more than you're ready to pay. I would do what I was not supposed to simply because it was the first time that I felt like I could. I never set out to become a dark figure, but for a while, that's what I was.

It all started out so innocently, wanting to live by some new means in which unconditional love was the key. As I stayed out in the night scene, the more I wanted to be part of the after party and kept on. Before I knew it, this involved late nights full of various drugs. I experienced the dark warmth of opiates, the chilling and triumphant highs of cocaine, the euphoric sensuality of ecstasy, even the strange organic world of psychedelic mushrooms and marijuana. I knew that my walking away from

Christianity and splitting up with my wife would cause a nasty backlash, so I put on my armor and made myself a beast. My security job at the club proved to be handy in giving me an outlet to my frustration and anger. I had never been in a fight before that period and learned what it was like to be in physical conflict.

People confronted me on my hypocrisy of leaving Christianity after being such a respected local advocate for it. I returned fire with absolute vitriol and bullish fury. I would pour every evil I knew them guilty of back on them and on many occasions threatened violence against them if they chose to really challenge me. In one case, my brother in law sent me a text, telling me to get back together with my estranged wife. He told me to "man up" and the discourse quickly became very heated.

Angry to the point of frenzy, I called him and got no answer. I left a message on his answering machine screaming at the top of my lungs that I was going to come down and bite his hypocritical nose off and swallow it so that he would never be able to show his face again. My sister called me, terrified by the things that I had said. I called my mother, who was not at all thrilled by my behavior and told her in tears that I wanted nothing more than to beat my brother in law to a messy pulp. In a moment that I admire her for, she gave me a motherly sense that I hadn't felt from her in years and brought me to a calm. I was shaking with anger and enraged at my brother in law, who, to me personified the height of Christian arrogance and blindness.

Big Man was my teacher in things I never knew, how to lie, how to get your money back from a thief and various other nefarious life skills. He provided me with the support I needed as I went through this confusion and helped me feel a little bit more stable as I walked through the abyss that those who lack any positive direction tread. With a landslide of people constantly telling me how horrible I was, my self-image was at an all time low. I was so hurt about so many things. I found out that cocaine could assuage my pain and I took solace in its temporary relief. With the divorce and my exit from Christianity, I had a double dose of sorrow. Sorrow at my failures, my guilt and the loss of innumerable friends. At that time, only a choice few were real friends to me.

Before I knew it, I found myself to be a part of a new group of friends who were fun and wild. They taught me how to buy and use cocaine and

I went for it with gusto! I embraced the drug culture as my new religion. When I was sad and lonely, I could change that feeling in moments. I'd pour a pile of that snow-white cocaine onto the mirror and crush it to make it smooth. I chopped it up into equidistant lines. In moments, I would go from the saddest person in the world to a rock star. My face and my emotions were numb and I felt like I could take on the world! All of my new friends were with me, so I rarely felt alone. We would stay out all night and have various adventures. We would sit in large groups together and share all kinds of drugs until dawn. It was something I had never experienced and yet it was like a church of another kind. We had a community, a meeting place, a communion-like breaking of bread. It was our little secret from the rest of world and it made me feel accepted.

Of course when the powder ran out and the beer was warm, the conversations waned. And as time passed, seeing the same people with the same problems every day created a great deal of depression. The highs were so high and so strong, but the lows split the hemispheres of my brain like a cold steel plate. The headaches were brutal and unrelenting and my emotions were absolutely volatile. My nose would become stuffy without any way of relief, except to consume more. It was the only time in my life in which I felt like I needed to do something, not just because I liked it, but because I needed it on a physical level. I knew that this was not a good thing. I wasn't making enough money at the club alone, so the next part was inevitable...I had to deal.

I learned the ways of a dealer and got in business with a few friends. I learned how to best protect myself from the eyes of the law and avoid detection. I developed my own methods of distribution through clever tricks. I met some really scary individuals who hid their operations in the most unlikely of places. Let's just say, that really bad people can be found hiding in the seemingly safest places.

There was a problem with my occupation as a dealer; I was too nice! I was like the drug dealer with the heart of gold, type of person. As my juiced up, weight lifting supplier would divvy out my goods, he would tell me about his time spent in The Bronx as a drug dealer. He detailed to me how he would cook up crack and mix in all sorts of household cleaners and intentionally sell it to people when he knew it could kill them. He also talked about how he often visited a crack house where they kept a naked woman chained to the floor at all times for anyone to use for a rock. This same person borrowed my SUV and headed to San Fransisco from Seattle one night. I got a call from him at 11pm saying my car had broken down on him and that he was at a casino in southern Oregon. He insisted that I come in his car and get him. He was crazy and had no problem killing people, so I didn't want to upset him. I got into his Mercedes and started my drive at midnight. I used my last bit of money to pick up a graham of cocaine for the road so that I would stay awake for the trip.

By the time I reached him, he was very drunk and angry, but was content enough that I had come to get him. I had not choice but to abandon the SUV on the side of the highway, because I was completely broke. I drove the car until we got outside of Sacramento where we switched off. I could only eat what he bought for me and had no idea where we were going, or what situation we might end up in. When we reached San Francisco, he told me that I couldn't come with him where he was going, so he gave me enough money for a one-way ticket on the B.A.R.T. train to Oakland. He gave me instructions on which stop to get off at. I was to meet some friends of his whom he said were very nice.

I took the stop and followed the directions that he gave me. After waiting an hour for the friends to come, they finally arrived. It turned out that they were a hippy lesbian couple. If you think that sounds nice, it wasn't nearly as nice as you might imagine. They took me to their apartment and began to chain smoke methamphetamine, something I had never taken, or ever planned to, but there I was. Although I didn't participate, I was stuck in their apartment for a day and a night with no food or money. It was strange to have no place to go, or means to get there. It was frightening to be at the mercy of the whim of someone capable of absolute cruelty.

As I waited for my supplier with the girls, a very fat man walked through the screen door unannounced and sat on their couch with them, keeping up a pleasant conversation while taking the crystalline shard and dropping it into his glass pipe. Once again, the room filled with the chemical smoke smell that only meth makes. I was high by proxy. I was too tired to enjoy any sort of upper, but was too tired to sleep. I got onto the girls computer and wrote on my social networking page, "SUV stranded on the side of the road in Oregon, stuck in San Francisco, oh well!". Meanwhile in the cyber world, my mother was watching my social networking posts with great scrutiny and passing on the latest dish of my hijinx to the rest of the family, to their horror.

My supplier finally returned and took me into San Francisco where we met with his friend who owned a strip club. They made some sort of deal in the back room of his apartment and we left with several baseball-sized chunks of Cocaine. We went to the grocery store and bought food. This wasn't for us to eat. We dug out the centers of the bread inside the packages and put the cocaine inside the hollows. When we were finished, they looked like perfectly new loafs of bread.

Because of my all night drive to San Fran and subsequent meth-hot boxing, I had not slept in nearly 48 hours. I drove in this condition over the pass in northern California. Only my absolute fear and discomfort being with a self-proclaimed killer and all around mad man kept me from falling asleep at the wheel through the foggy and treacherous mountain pass into southern Oregon and on to Washington state. After this trip, I realized there was no glamour or longevity in a life of heavy drug use. I asked myself: How have I become connected with such awful people in such a short period of time? I saw where entry-level narcotic use takes you and didn't like what I saw. From that point on, I did my best to escape from the relationships I had with people who I knew through drug association.

Why had I gone down this path? What was I thinking? The ups were never worth the downs and the women were just the same in this manner. I found myself in poverty most of the time, surrounded by people who would not let me rest because they were doing or pursuing drugs. I was in a desperate state of loneliness, lost and out of control. I behaved like trash because that was how I felt about myself. I had escaped the unhappiness that consumed me in Christianity and found a pain that was deeper and darker greeting me in this new world. Was I like the prodigal son of the Bible, or was I simply doing the right thing in the wrong way?

Unfortunately, I had very few people who would speak kindly to me. The rest of my friends and family had nothing to say to me. All their answers were canned Christian answers and that just didn't cut it like they did in the past. But I felt like trash, so I acted like trash; I answered their rebukes with violent retorts. Was this really all I was meant to be? Was I fulfilling every naysayer's prophecy about me? I had to decide for myself that I and I alone had to make the choice to change for good. I had to find a way to grow and not wallow in the sadness I was mired in.

It was then that I started working for my brother, who had a construction company. It was good to do wholesome work with my big brother. He had gone through his own tumults, but had come out living a pretty responsible life. I knew that I could get out of the world I fell into if I really gave it my all. My father also played a strong part in reminding me that my story was not over. But making your way out of a lifestyle in the drug culture is hard.

I had to take things one day at a time. I had successfully ditched the bad influence of drug addicted girlfriends and gangster types and was working towards using my degree to find a respectable office job of some sort.

After my separation from the drug scene, Big Man took out his frustrations on me, because I was no longer around when I used to always be his right hand man. He started to behave more and more erratic and strange, upset that I would never hang around anymore. It all came to a head when I received an early morning call from him; he had taken a bottle of anti-anxiety pills.

For his privacy I will not share the rest of the story, but will share that I was luckily able to get him to the hospital. He was not however happy with the circumstances I had confronted him with after his recovery and he came after me on a rampage. I heard from a friend that he was looking for me and sounded angry. I wasn't sure where to go or what to do. Before I knew it, I could hear the telltale steps of his large frame at my doorstep. I went to hide wherever I could, but our house was small, with little place for myself to hide since I myself am six foot five. I busted into a roommates room where his pet pitbull was resting. I slid behind the door hoping that the dog would not give away my presence. Big man came through the door asking my roommate where I was, "I don't know, he was just here" he replied. Just then and without notice, the door I stood behind slammed open and roused the dog from her slumber.

Luckily I was just skinny enough for the door to slam into the wall instead of hitting me, thus giving away my position. I stood there, afraid to breathe, terrified for my life. But it was not to be over so easily. Big Man sat down on the couch with my roommate and proceeded to talk to him about how I had been causing problems and listing off all of my shortcomings. Not realizing how out of context he might have been having just been released from the hospital for the anti-anxiety overdose incident. After what felt like hours, he left to look for me elsewhere. I waited for an extra 15 minutes behind the door before I called for my roommate. He was astonished that I indeed had been there the whole time, hiding behind the door. It was clear to us both that Big Man was out for violence against me in his unstable state. After a little more time had passed, I headed out to a place where one of my best friends was working. I was too scared to stay at home and too scared to go anywhere else that was less public.

Over and over my phone would ring with Big Man on the other line. Forward to voicemail, forward to voicemail. Finally I couldn't take the ringing anymore and answered the phone. Big Man asked me where I was and I replied that I didn't want to talk to him in person because I thought he wanted to hurt me. Unfortunately, all he needed to know was the general area I was in. Not ten minutes later, Big Man entered the restaurant whose bar I was sitting at. I was drinking water, being too afraid to take a single drink of anything that might slow my mind in this tense period of time.

Big Man made his way to me at the end of the bar and said, "You don't wanna talk to me!?" Before I could reply, his massive fist came across my jaw and temple, knocking me silly. I recovered from the first blow in just enough time for blow number two which knocked me to the floor. Being cold cocked by a man 5 inches taller and 100lbs my better was not an easy feat to survive without being knocked out. I curled up into a ball against the wall while the manager jumped out and yelled at Big Man to leave before the cops get called. My pal working at the bar just stood in total shock at the scene he had just witnessed. Luckily, the size of Big Man's fist distributed the blow along enough of my face that it didn't break any bones, but my emotions were at an all time high. I got back up and had myself a whiskey sour to quell the oncoming pain that began to radiate with more and more fire. That night, my roommates and I all slept with weapons in our hands for fear of another attack. This was the final straw for me. The violence and craziness that comes with narcotics was all too real to me. I was watching it turn good people like Big Man into temporary monsters and had myself become a monster at times.

I had to change my life and figure out where to

go from here. My heart was so empty without the feeling I had as a Christian, that no matter how dark things got, Jesus was there for me. Now I didn't have that reassurance. I didn't know what would happen to me. It was then that I realized that I was the only person who could change my situation. I didn't have a new spiritual advisor to fit me perfectly into some new system of belief. I had to do this for me. The heartache and pain that I caused myself and others during this dark year may have been avoided if I had developed some other faith system, but ultimately I believe this time was a strong learning experience for me. It taught me that people are the same everywhere.

I saw how a drug circle is like a church of its own, with its disciples and devotees. We looked at each other like we belonged to something that was beyond the norm. When this happened, it replaced the community that I felt in church. My church was that of shadows and dark deeds, but it had its allure of coolness. My devotees were looking for answers just like people in any religious setting. I saw the ugly side of it as well; the eventual turn that people take when they reach a crossroads in their life. Do they decide to become what they vowed never to be; a vagrant, a prostitute, a drug addict. Was that the way they wanted to be known by their friends, their family, even their children. I had to face this question as well and luckily was able to make the right decision; I chose life. Sadly, this isn't what all of my friends chose.

There is something in life we all need to be a part of. We cannot run through this life without some sort of motivator. We have this unrelenting propensity to want to classify others and ourselves. Perhaps it is some part of the way we are raised in this society, or perhaps it's in our genetics. Either way, we need it like we need love. There is a dark romance that people in the drug culture have; a way of doing things and behaving that makes it almost like film noir. The ritual of doing the drug has its own mystery and romance; just like when you get up and drink a cup of coffee in the morning, you don't just have coffee.

You walk into the kitchen, turn on the light, open that bag or can and catch a whiff of it as you pour the grounds into the coffee machine. Perhaps you heat up the water and stand there in the morning light listening to the water in the teakettle build up and race around within until it comes to a high-pressured whistle. You pour the water and watch it turn to black gold.

Drug people do it the same way; they pick up their bag, they get to a safe place for their ritual. Perhaps they pull and break up the chunks into a fine powder, or heat it under a spoon, readying it for a needle. This one thing is something they are the masters of, the one thing in their life they can control. If you understand that, perhaps you can understand that people in this situation are not all monsters. They are real people who have fallen into a sadness that everyday life was not healing; they are the ghosts of our society while still being alive. They saw it coming at some pivotal point in their drug use, where they just decided to give in one more time. Sometimes their dark year turns into a dark life. Even worse, as in the case of my friend Bobby, it turned into a dark death. I consider the end of my dark year to be the day I heard he had passed from a heroin overdose. I feel it is appropriate to share with you something he wrote for a friend of his who passed;

Eli
I found out yesterday that a long time friend of mine died from cancer theday before, he was 24 years old. That night I took a few sleeping pills to go to sleep quickly as I could, and avoid thoughts

and being alone as much as possible. I dreamt about birds...I woke up to a gray day, and I am grateful for that. If it had been bright and clear it wouldn't have felt right. The day allowed me to quietly think and feel the things that come. Eli was a tough kid.

I always had a certain sense about going into it with him even if we were sure to lose, I felt okay. I was glad he was there. And I remember myself and us as a whole being outnumbered again and saying,"Man, I wish Eli was here." Luckily, it wasn't often he wasn't there. I'd be doomed...Why God, do I befriend the scrawniest bunch of misfits with the biggest mouths around? fuckin' skate rats. But afterward we'd be drinking and laughing even if we were bloody, and wounded...talking like we win no matter what. Eli could hold his own and then some. He was never afraid. Man, I wish Eli was here.

And I feel the same way for Bobby. He overdosed in New York City in the winter of my rebirth. One time at a party, Bobby kept to himself in the corner of the room, sadness glowing off him like a dark spotlight. I asked him what the problem was and he simply looked at me with his signature hound dog eyes and said he knew he was going to die as a junkie. I told him with tears in my eyes that it didn't need to happen, that he could be anything he wanted to be and do anything he wanted to do. That was 2 years before he overdosed.

After Bobby's passing, I knew the story of my life needed to be very different. I needed to do well, not just for myself, but also in honor of his memory. It was too soon and so unnecessary for him to go.

I went into the darkness because I thought it was the only option; there was good and there was evil. I had not yet moved on from my black and white ideology. I take full responsibility for my behavior during my darkest days, but I also recognize that I knew nothing of the world before I went through it. I only saw the idealized version of everything. I'm not saying that anyone else should go through what I did, because it is destructive and deadly, but the only way I can redeem that time is to learn from it.
The dark year is not an actual calendar year; it is a state of mind, a place in which you give up and let the rain wash you into the gutter. It is a sense of freedom in its own way, but of course that freedom comes with a heavy price. This is the place where you hide from your sadness and

grief; it's where you can somehow become something that you are not. It's a rock and roll story of your own in which even the dead junkies are heroes, because you know they were actual people with a dismal beauty of their own. They are your people and you understood them as comrades in sorrow. But we are meant for something more than this and joy is far better shared among living friends than over a grave. And so, my dark year came to an end.

THE SCIENCE OF REBIRTH

We all know about the cooling of steam into water and the cooling of water into ice crystals, as in snowflakes and frost. This formative process occurs as thermal chaos is reduced. The opposite happens if you warm things up. So there seems to be an inverse relationship between chaos and form. In a sense, that's what's happened to the entire universe. – Rupert Sheldrake, from the book, "Chaos, Creativity and Cosmic Consciousness"

With Christianity at my back and an unknown future ahead, I felt the thirst for knowledge overtake me. I opened myself up in ways that I never had before and started to listen to non-biblical teachings for the first time in my life. What did it mean to be one with the universe? What did it mean when people said that God is everything and we are God? These were questions that I wanted answers to. I didn't know how I thought of God now I didn't have a manual on the matter, so where could I go from here?

I read a book by the Dalai Lama called, "The Universe In A Single Atom". In this book, he detailed the dangers and advantages of scientific discovery in the face of the ancient Buddhist faith. He said things that astonished me and challenged my conceptions of what faith could look like. Consider this phrase for instance:

If, when we investigate something, we find there is reason and proof for it, we must acknowledge that as reality-even if it is in contradiction with a literal scriptural explanation that has held sway for many centuries or with a deeply held opinion or view. So one fundamental attitude shared by Buddhism and science is the commitment to keep searching for reality by empirical means and to be willing to discard accepted or long held positions if our search finds that the truth is different.

I had never held this stance before as a Christian, but was now ready to adopt this idea in my new search for truth. I may no longer have been a Christian, but this was because I knew that it was not the whole truth. In my experience, the whole truth is not found in one single organized religion, but many truths can be understood and applied in one's life through the integration of what we can find to be empirical. Even among these great teachings and the advances in science, we are still required to believe in that which is mystical in nature. I embrace this idea, but want to refine what I know through empirical evidence and personal experience to develop a faith that is my own. One that brings me closer to knowing the true nature of God and man. For all my years, I thought that scientists were some sort of gang of smarties who were out to destroy the image of God, so they could live unethical lives. When I realized how silly this notion was, I was able to look into what they said. As a result, I have been filled with a greater sense of awe and marvel for the universe and its creation than ever before.

Let's take a curious gland in the center of your brain as an initial example of science leading the way to my spiritual rebirth. The pineal gland is a pine nut sized and shaped gland that sits in the very center of our brains. It is separate from the brain and in fetal development actually grows from the roof of the mouth. It's purposes are not fully known, however we know that it produces melatonin, the natural chemical that helps to induce sleep and stimulate our dream state. It also generates a powerful psychedelic chemical called Dimethyltryptamine, or DMT for short. It's other curious features include the fact that it is the only organ in the brain cavity that is not actually part of the brain. It is the only part of the brain cavity that is not split into hemispheres. We know that when a person's body dies, it is the last part of the body to continue its function and in fact works harder at this time than any other time in the life of that body. In his book, "DMT: The Spirit Molecule" Rick Strassman M.D. has presented extremely strong evidence that this tiny gland is as Rene Descartes concluded, "the seat of the soul". In fact this tiny gland has the same optic nerves, cornea and retina that our eyes have and is widely regarded as the third eye.

Ancient Hindu and Egyptian faiths have known this and promulgated these beliefs in their religious rites. Here we see the evidence of spiritual truth that has been revealed by science. In my case, I didn't believe in the third eye until I saw the scientific evidence behind it. Now that I am equipped with this understanding, I can take this into account when I make decisions about what I should or should not believe. Let us now consider the unfathomable order in which the universe is operating. Take for instance, the strange case of the poles of the planet Saturn. On each pole, the cloud forms make a hexagonal shape! Polarity of the planet forces the clouds of gas to make this geometric shape. The images are readily found in a Google.com search.

We know from scientific studies that particles jump in and out of existence constantly and that this occurs in every particle in existence. That's right, every particle that makes you and me is popping in and out of existence right now. That means that they are going somewhere, but to where? We can only speculate.

We know from research and extensive use by the military that remote viewing works. Remote viewing requires no religious preconditions and simply requires that a person relax and think of an object elsewhere and describe what they see when their eyes are closed. The United States Government has used these skills for decades now. I have personally experienced this working at home with basic experimentation. The primary lesson of remote viewing is the concept of non-locality, which is the idea that all things everywhere are singularly connected to you on some deeper level. We are literally next to everyone and everything in space and time. Space and time, from a scientific standpoint are only units of measurement in our present perception and not wholly accurate to the full reality in which we live. That being said, things that happened in the past are present now in some way and so are the things in the future. The greatest part of non-locality is the realization that we as humans are all directly connected to one another right here and now.

You and I at this very moment are wholly connected to the entire universe; we simply have too small a capacity to grasp it within this body. When we understand this, we realize that we are one. Based on these proven concepts, which you could easily practice at home and discover, I have come to realize what was meant by the ancient teachers of old who claimed that they were one with God and that God was them. It made sense to me that all things are God. In his book, "Limitless Mind" Russell Targ says this about the reality of non-locality:

John Clauser (with Stuart Freedman) at the university of California at Berkeley, was the first to demonstrate non-locality in the laboratory. He recently described to me his first impressions of these experiments, saying, "Quantum experiments have been carried out with twin photons, electrons, atoms, and even large atomic structures such as 60-carbon atom Bucky balls. It may be impossible to keep anything in a box anymore"

Again we see that ancient ideas about being everywhere and nowhere all at once are now a scientific reality. This has been taught for thousands of years in various eastern faiths! This has been one of the most important findings to me anywhere, because it makes me responsible for myself as a part of the whole universe.

If I look inside myself, I can see that I am made up of organs that are made of cells, which are made of atoms, which are made of protons and electrons, which are made of quarks. When I look to something bigger, I am a part of the body of the earth, which is a body of the solar system, which is a body of the Milky Way, which is a part of a galaxy cluster, which is a tiny dot in the sea of the universe. Either direction I look, I am wholly connected in a real, scientific and spiritual way. When this really sunk in, it changed my drive for materialism and selfishness (on which I'm still working). But, oh the journey of discovery this has led me to!

When we think about the example given in the quote at the beginning of this chapter, we can see the amazing organization that seemingly occurs out of chaos. The steam turns to water as it cools. Water is a more complex molecular body than steam. Then as the water continues to cool, it becomes even more complex. Why is this important? It is a basic example that anywhere we look in the universe, we don't just see a stand still portrait of creation, but indeed we see new creation every day. To me this is both a scientific revelation that guides me directly to an intelligent and beautiful creator and a wonderful metaphor for us as individuals.

We are a part of this ongoing creation ourselves. We can see mutation in the strains of viruses. For example, it is likely that you have had, or will soon have a cold. We know that you never get the same cold twice. This occurs because the cold virus mutates. So we see the evolutionary process in everything, including colds, unfortunately! Now that we are out of the woods of living in fear about fighting the evolution vs. creation fight, we can enjoy these simple examples for the truth they hold.

This has brought me to a belief that we are totally connected, evolving spiritually and personally and are one with God. Coming to this conclusion was what brought my joy back to me. Since I know that God exists in myself and everyone and everything, I must do my best to have reverence and respect and most importantly, love for everyone. Take a moment right now and think about what it really means to be connected spiritually and physically to everyone and everything. How does that change the way you feel as you consider this? Does it make you want to empty out your hatred and fear; does it fill you with a greater compassion for those you may have considered your enemies? It's something I consider to be one of the biggest revelations of my life. The application of it has given me a deeper love of God and humanity that I never had before.

MYSTIC MESSIAH

I say by Nut, the brilliant, the great: This is my son, my first born, opener of my womb; this is my beloved, with whom I have been satisfied. – 2400-2300 BC Ancient Pyramid Texts, Hymn 1

The life of Jesus is one of the most debated, celebrated and argued subjects of all time. What can be said about someone who changed the face of the world by his presence? At times, Jesus showed supreme compassion and love, at other times he claimed to be God himself. I'd like to discuss some aspects of his life and existence that seem to be little talked about. If you have followed so far, you will not need this chapter to definitively tell you whether or not Jesus was the Son of God, sacrificed to save your soul, but this book would be incomplete without direct attention given to Jesus. No matter what you believe about him, his life was full of mystery and magic and life lessons that we can all benefit from without necessarily believing him to be God incarnate in the fashion that the New Testament paints him.

Very little time is really spent giving detail to the beginnings and upbringing of Jesus. We are almost expected to gloss over it without a thought, but this era is full of mystery and amazing possibility and should be examined with a little more thought in order to ascertain how Jesus became the ageless figure we know him as today.

Let's start from the second chapter of the Gospel of Matthew (NIV)

After Jesus was born in Bethlehem in Judea, during the time of King Herod, Magi from the east came to Jerusalem and asked, "Where is the one who has been born king of the Jews? We saw his star when it rose and have come to worship him."

When King Herod heard this he was disturbed, and all Jerusalem with him. When he had called together all the people's chief priests and teachers of the law, he asked them where the Messiah was to be born. "In Bethlehem in Judea," they replied, "for this is what the prophet has written:

"'But you, Bethlehem, in the land of Judah, are by no means least among the rulers of Judah; for out of you will come a ruler who will shepherd my people Israel.'"

Then Herod called the Magi secretly and found out from them the exact time the star had appeared. He sent them to Bethlehem and said, "Go and search carefully for the child. As soon as you find him, report to me, so that I too may go and worship him."

After they had heard the king, they went on their way, and the star they had seen when it rose went ahead of them until it stopped over the place where the child was. When they saw the star, they were overjoyed. On coming to the house, they saw the child with his mother Mary, and they bowed down and worshiped him. Then they opened their treasures and presented him with gifts of gold, frankincense and myrrh. And having been warned in a dream not to go back to Herod, they returned to their country by another route.

The story is well known, but the first thing that we notice is the presence of the Magi. Who were these Magi from the east? Since the Bible puts them front and center, they must have had special significance, because they are the first point of validation of the kingship of Jesus, or his extremely special nature. Since the fourth century BC, the Magi were generally considered adepts of the great Persian alchemist and magician, Zoroaster. This singular detail brings up a question of spiritual authority, which we covered earlier;

By whose power do these people operate, by God or by Satan? If by God, then does this validate the use of magic in the Zoroastrian tradition? And if by the devil, then why would their presence be allowed to stain the pages of the Holy Bible?

This is an important question for Christians to ask because the Magi are absolutely foundational in the initial validation of Jesus as the Christ. According to Old Testament law, witchcraft, divination and alchemy are all forbidden and yet we have the adepts of Zoroaster front and center in the life of little baby Jesus.

Let's look at this from a philosophical standpoint and imagine what it would be like to be the Magi searching for this newborn king. The Magi were of enough renown to have audience with King Herod and were obviously very advanced in their knowledge of astrology. If the Magi stopped everything they were doing to follow a star and find this new king, would they not possibly bring gifts that instilled their vast and ancient magical knowledge? Doesn't it seem unlikely that they would only bring fine oils, incense and treasures to a world-changing king? It seems highly plausible that these Magi would bring magical texts for the young king that would educate him in their ways. When we later see the miracles that Jesus performs, it makes sense. He demonstrated a vast understanding of, not just the world as the Jews of that time saw it, but of eastern and Egyptian thought. With this in mind, let's take a look at the next pivotal event in the life of young Jesus;

When they had gone, an angel of the Lord appeared to Joseph in a dream. "Get up," he said, "take the child and his mother and escape to Egypt. Stay there until I tell you, for Herod is going to search for the child to kill him."
So he got up, took the child and his mother during the night and left for Egypt, where he stayed until the death of Herod. And so was fulfilled what the Lord had said through the prophet: "Out of Egypt I called my son."

From this point on, Jesus is raised in Egypt, the home of the very first monotheistic religion in the world. If you look at the quote from the Pyramid text at the beginning of this chapter, you see a familiar concept, "this is my son...in whom I am well pleased"
The Egyptian theology is a keystone of the life of

Jesus. Concepts of being reborn and being a singular son of a monotheistic God were traditions of Egyptian thought long before Jesus was born. Any short study into the life of Pharaohs will reveal this fact. Egyptian Pharaoh Akhenaten who ruled around 1340 BC claimed to be the Son of Aten, the God of Gods. When you look at the parallel between Osiris and Jesus, the similarities in concepts of rebirth, victory over the grave and being Lord of the afterlife are quite compelling. So now Jesus is perfectly placed in the presence of the ancient Magi and is now living in Egypt, the ancient home of religion. Jesus lived in Egypt until the age of twelve, returning to Israel after King Herod died.

Now imagine this for a moment, you are Jesus. You've been told the story of your birth and the visitation of the Magi and being of the Hebrew faith, you've been read the prophecies about the messiah. You've likely received ancient and special knowledge from the Magi. They would have equipped you to the best of their understanding.

Let's think about this seriously for a moment. If you were told you were going to be the savior of the world, wouldn't you do everything you could to learn the great teachings of the east and Egypt, especially if those teachings were placed in your lap? With these details in hand, it seems to point to Jesus having access to Egyptian and Persian teachings in the area of magic. Jesus' life and times were important astrological events that both Persian and Egyptian astrologers would undoubtedly recognize as very important. Many aspects of Jesus' life were beyond his control. He could not, for instance, choose where he was born, or by whom he was born of. In traditional Christian teaching, we've glossed over some very important aspects of his life and have built a belief system out of it.

When we witness the amazing works that modern magicians can perform, we know that they are not God, even though their deeds are often otherworldly. We know that there are healers in every religious tradition in every corner of the world, from witch doctors in Africa, to psychic surgeons in Mexico and even faith healers in Christian traditions. In this day and age, we have a mixture of all of the things that Christ did, even resurrection from the grave.
When we consider the experiences that Jesus went through during his 40 days in the desert, we see a common theme in the transformative process of any great spiritual leader. As I have described before, shamans and medicine men go

through a harrowing wilderness experience in which they are carted into a spirit world and exposed to all forms of torture at the hands of strange beings. In the fourth chapter of The Gospel of Matthew we see Jesus going through this experience;

Then Jesus was led by the Spirit into the wilderness to be tempted by the devil. After fasting forty days and forty nights, he was hungry. The tempter came to him and said, "If you are the Son of God, tell these stones to become bread."
Jesus answered, "It is written: 'Man shall not live on bread alone, but on every word that comes from the mouth of God.'"

At the very beginning of this chapter, we see that Jesus is led by the spirit to be tempted by the devil. This denotes a pre-meditated plan to go through his vetting process as a spiritual leader. The fact that he fasted for 40 days also is of great importance. As I said before, one of the ways in which a shaman comes to a great spiritual state is through austerity. Through starvation and absolute submission to the spirit world, a leader shows his reverence for the realm beyond and is submitted to whatever torture is set before them. This is not a coincidence, but is a tradition that Jesus would have known of from his understanding of Persian and Egyptian wisdom in the realm of magic. In this state he is brought face to face with the great tempter and must get through these tests before fully coming to his own as a spiritual master. Roughly 500 years prior to the arrival of Jesus, another great spiritual leader went through this same universal process that many spiritual greats go through.

In the story of the Buddha, Siddhartha refused to leave the base of the bodhi tree under which he was meditating until he had reached enlightenment. Here in this state of self-refusal and deep meditation, Siddhartha was also confronted with the pleasures of the world, offered the kingdoms of the world, but Siddhartha refused it all, knowing that all of these offers were illusory. The devil of East Indian culture, Mara displayed all of these temptations before Buddha. Only after Siddhartha was forced to look at and deny his very ego was he able to reach enlightenment. So here, these world-changing spiritual leaders are led along a parallel path before truly beginning their spiritual work. In each case, the leader is capable of many glorious miracles and healings and supernatural power of every sort. There is a primary difference between Siddhartha and Jesus though;

only Jesus claimed to be God. In John 8:53-59 we see this claim with clarity;

(The Pharisees said) Are you greater than our father Abraham? He died, and so did the prophets. Who do you think you are?"

Jesus replied, "If I glorify myself, my glory means nothing. My Father, whom you claim as your God, is the one who glorifies me. Though you do not know him, I know him. If I said I did not, I would be a liar like you, but I do know him and obey his word. Your father Abraham rejoiced at the thought of seeing my day; he saw it and was glad."

"You are not yet fifty years old," they said to him, "and you have seen Abraham!"

"Very truly I tell you," Jesus answered, "before Abraham was born, I am!" At this, they picked up stones to stone him, but Jesus hid himself, slipping away from the temple grounds.

The significance comes when he says, "before Abraham was born, I AM". This is because he says the word for God, a word that was unlawful to say directly. He directly said that he was God. From my perspective, it's easy to understand how Jesus came to believe this. His life was started with the appearance of the greatest wise men of the age worshipping him; he was raised with this knowledge and an otherworldly gift to accomplish great deeds and miracles and everywhere he went, people gathered behind him.

In short, I believe that Jesus really thought he was God, but what he really meant upon this proclamation was not fully clear at the time of his crucifixion. Another valuable thought in this discussion is the idea that Jesus simply knew that we were all God in the sense that we were an extension of the sensory portion of the ethereal God and he was to be our patriarch of this realization. Like drops of water in the ocean, Jesus understood that he was both a drop of water in the ocean of God and as a drop in the ocean was also the ocean itself.

This dual message is very Gnostic in nature and was way too advanced for its time in the west, though accepted broadly in other cultures of the east. Robert Bauval & Graham Hancock had this to say about the Gnostics in their book, The Master Game:

In 1945 a great hoard of hitherto unknown Gnostic texts from the early centuries of the Christian era was found at Nag Hammadi in Upper Egypt. Since the translation and eventual publication of these texts in 1977 it has become apparent that Christianity's relationship with Gnosticism goes back to the very beginnings of the Christian cult in the first century AD. Likewise, it is now obvious, and widely accepted, that, 'Christian Gnosticism' was not some offshoot from the mainstream of Christianity. On the contrary it was part of the mainstream- perhaps even the major part.

If Gnosticism was part of the mainstream of Christianity, why don't we know about them or incorporate their thoughts in modern Christian doctrine? Robert Bauval and Graham Hancock continue:

And then something happened. From the beginning of the fourth century AD, as it acquired state power, the Church undertook a radical change in direction. The freethinking and sometimes anarchical approach of Gnostics began to be frowned upon, their allegorical interpretations of the scriptures were dropped in favor of literal ones, and persecutions for heresy began almost immediately.

A little history shows us that the side of Christianity that we see today is the side that won out by literally killing off the other side. The victor writes history and so it has been even in Christendom. By 325 AD, the Council of Nicea had put together the Bible the way they wanted it to be and excluded Gnostic theology and teachings; teachings that painted Jesus in a much more eastern light. What did the Gnostics believe that was so different? The Gnostics believed that the God of the Old Testament was an evil demigod and not the true God of spirit. They believed that the physical world was a literal hell and that the flesh was doomed to pull the real you into perdition forever. They practiced extreme austerities and denied themselves any sort of pleasure, knowing that it would lead them towards more fleshly desires. In essence, they were devout believers that Jesus came to show us an example of how to live this life; that he was a phantasm of the true God of creation.

They believe that his death and resurrection were to simply show us his power and might as an illustration of God's victory over the fleshly world. The Gnostics were against violence and were therefore easy to kill and persecute once the Christian church had the spears of Rome at its disposal.

And so we see that there was more than one perspective on the Old Testament, a Gnostic Christian perspective that in my mind more closely reflects what our sensible humanitarian natures are agreeable to. One perspective says that the God of the Old Testament is the same as the God of the New Testament. This is the traditional view based on what has been passed down, first in Catholicism and now to Protestantism. The other view is just as relevant if you wish to be a purist about who Christians really were in the first 3 centuries of its existence. This is the view that the God of the Old Testament was indeed a blood soaked monster who wished to enslave humanity in subservience and reverence to him. This makes sense when you see words like 'Jealous' repeated in Old Testament prophecy and scripture. These traits seem all too human to be truly divine.

However we believe it, Jesus' claim was in a context that was unacceptable to the powers that were, and this was the reason why they eventually sent him to the cross. After this statement, Jesus knew that he would die as a martyr, but did he perhaps still have the upper hand? Was he, as the greatest real magician of all time capable of performing the ultimate act by surviving the crucifixion?

I know that this may be a hard idea to swallow, but if you look today at the works of street magicians, you can see feats similar to these. Popular magicians like Criss Angel can perform amazing feats that are astonishingly Christ-like in potency. You can see him walk on water with people all around him. You can even see him get run over by a steamroller while lying on a bed of broken glass. Imagine now that a person of this skill level could do all of these things in reality. If you look at the nature of his beginnings, I think that you can understand how this is possible.

Imagine that Jesus was a true healer in the shamanic respect and a Magi in his understanding of himself in the timing and placement within the universal order. Imagine all of those traits all held in one man who truly thought that he was God in a sense that was completely foreign at the time, even to his own disciples. If this were really the case, then what seems impossible, the survival of a Roman crucifixion is possible and in his case, probable.

After his greatest feat, his disciples who learned many of his ways and understanding were able to perform similar miracles and deeds by the same understanding. This was all a proof to them that Jesus was truly that he said he was. They believed in him so strongly that many became martyrs for this belief. Though many often associate it with the most pious of ways to die, we must understand that martyrdom is not proof of truth. If that were the case, then extreme Islamic suicide bombings would be proving their beliefs to be true.

I believe that the very best guess about the source of Jesus' power was ancient magic from Persian and Egyptian sources, or that he was as the Gnostics said. It is my strong opinion that Jesus could have easily been an adept of the magic and teachings of the Magi and a learned and naturally skilled shaman, evidentially the greatest that ever lived. This is how he accomplished everything he did. This also meshes very well with Gnostic concept that Jesus was actually a far advanced incorporeal being that materialized in order to perfect his process of becoming one with God fully as the creative force and best example of our own eventual journey to oneness.

Salvation in the traditional western Christian view

is necessary because we are guilty criminals in the court of God. The crucifixion represents the suffering and death that Jesus underwent to acquit us of our condemnation. To the Gnostic, the crucifixion was a gory horror that should not have been flaunted as by their competitors of the early church. The waving of the cross, to them was a new form of idolatry that held people firmly in the evil demigod's world of fleshly distraction, worrying about the tearing and destruction of the body and not the message of freedom.

To the Gnostics the crucifixion was the final representation of what we can accomplish if we follow Christ's lead. In other words, the real God that Jesus represents in the Gnostic mind is one who wants peers, while the traditional western Christian God wants groveling supplicants and slaves. In a moment that often is overlooked, Jesus himself tells us which he prefers in John 15:15 (NIV): I no longer call you servants, because a servant does not know his master's business. Instead, I have called you friends, for everything that I learned from my Father I have made known to you.
In this passage, Jesus relates us as equals, not as slaves or underlings. I've already explained the difference between what it means to be a part of

God, therefore to be God, yet not be God in the entire sense. This mindset brings encouragement, reverence and motivation to me while freeing my mind from the burden of fear brought on by the evil demi-god of the Old Testament. If you can follow that thought, then you can understand how Jesus Christ relates to us with world changing power without the greatest guilt trip ever laid on humanity by the western Christian version of the story.

In the Far East, there are great masters, who even after they have lived and died still provide guidance to spiritual seekers today. Jesus is considered to be one of the greatest masters of all time in this spiritual respect and appears to people of every religion around the world. There are many other ways in which we can speculate about how Jesus did what he did, but the stars did not lie when they guided the Magi. We know this assuredly because we are still talking about him today. People still worship him as God, but with a misunderstanding of the nature of God and our place with God. Indeed, there is much to be learned from the life of Jesus, but it does not necessarily mean that he was the Son of God in the way the New Testament claims.

Finally, you only need Jesus to be the Son of

God, sacrificed for your sins if you buy into the rest of the biblical text being the inerrant word of God. I have already presented the evidence, both empirically and philosophically to bring serious doubt to the concept biblical concept of sin, salvation and hell. But when you see his deeds and his great teachings, they should be appreciated and applied as your heart guides you along your own spiritual path. Jesus might have been like a stone thrown into still water, causing ripples in every direction. His disciples being close to him rode the wave of his power and eventually losing His essence as the years made the ripples smaller and smaller, ran with their version of his story until the water again became stagnant in the mire of human error and the collection of earthly power.

A NEW LIFE

There are fleeting moments in my life in which everything is beautiful, a still portrait in a time of bliss. These moments almost always involve someone I love. There might not be any form of sexuality or high-gloss glamour at the moment, but the real beauty overflows and peels back the veneer of my own trained artificiality; showing the banal world I've accepted for the illusion that it is. In that instance, I see a glimpse of how life could be. When I am in that special moment, perhaps on a road trip, or simply spending time with friends, I feel that symbiotic energy flowing through me, calling me to stay there in that moment. Why can't it always be like that singular moment? Perhaps it depends on what we willing to do to get there.

Perhaps we should begin by peeling away all falsehood from ourselves, observing the world around us with sober minded discretion to discern the real from the fake. This means taking a hard look at what we have learned and being willing to ask ourselves what needs to change.

This is a process that I went through as I moved on from Christianity into a new life. As we've seen, it's not an easy process at all, but we cannot live in fear of the boogeyman of falsehood. It would have been easy to just give up and let destruction take me over, despairing that I couldn't call upon some higher power to save me. Ultimately I feel it was God's intention that I make my own way out and learn the new path that I must tread. I was responsible for my failures, my victories, and myself. Even though I realized that the gospel as I knew it was false, I still wanted to cling to it, for it was all I knew of any concept of good. But, we don't need to be afraid to let go of that which isn't true and so I did let go.

So in this new journey of truth seeking, we must put down the baggage of our old ways that do not work. It's only then that we can sit before the blank canvas of our spirituality and begin a new creation wholly based on our love, heartfelt convictions and compassion.

I believe that the Bible has innumerable lessons for us all and that they should be taught, but I also believe that investing our minds and hearts into a concept that is greatly flawed and emotionally destructive is not acceptable. There is a heaven that we cannot fathom and we can see a glimpse of it in many ways now; how you see it is part of your journey. There is also a hell that we experience now; it is a state of mind, which traps you in fear, perhaps it is the world of the evil demi-god. The contest of sin, salvation and hell is a false contest, one that puts you in turmoil. Those who accept this prison of religious dogma often are content to live their lives within it, but few ever see the bliss that they could experience in a life of fearless discovery.

New life is possible and is yours to take if you are willing to do the hard work of rebuilding yourself. You are not alone, many before you have made this journey and are more joyful because of it. The universe is full of mystery and beauty that can be seen, unstained by the gore and violence of demi-god of the Bible as we know it.

I believe that there is a God and that his core nature is love. When we experience love, we are experiencing a taste of God's divine nature. But I'm not here to tell you what to believe; you must take the initiative to use your heart and mind to judge the true from the false. If we decide to put aside all that is false and remove these aspects from ourselves on a daily basis, we will have truth as our guide.

The truth is like a diamond within coal; it is there, sparkling and unbreakable, hiding within the dross; it wants to be found, to shine for all who behold it. We are lucky that truth is more present than diamonds; it is freely there for anyone willing to get their hands dirty. Now that I am no longer willing to view the world from the prejudice of my former dogma, I can look for the real truth everywhere I go. The truth does not care who speaks it, it only cares to be spoken and so we listen to everyone to find our precious treasure of truth. In the process, we become more adept at finding the truth, for we know its flawless character.

But what do we do in the meantime as we build our new life from scratch? How then should we carry ourselves in this life? We must start with the basics:

Love unconditionally
Forgive unconditionally
Seek the truth wherever it may be found

What does life look like when we love unconditionally? Consider for a moment how it might change you if you really woke up every day with this on your mind. You know we are all connected and that in essence everyone else is an extension of you. When you love them, you love a piece of yourself. Imagine now how the world would look if everyone woke up in the morning thinking this way. Do you think that our generals would command our soldiers to pick up their weapons and go to war?

Would corporations only look at the bottom line of an accounting spreadsheet, or would they look at the impact of their business on people and the world in which we live? Would we say hurtful things to people? Would we see the world solve most of its problems in months, weeks, or even days? I believe in unconditional love. I believe Jesus spoke rightly when he spoke of it and believe that it is the unifying factor in all religions.

Think of the venerable Mother Theresa who dedicated her life to serving the lost children of Calcutta India for her entire life. Now imagine if the whole world was full of Mother Theresa's. Imagine the unbelievable kindness that we would bestow on each other if we always thought this way. I believe those special moments that we have too few of in our lives could become normal life in a world of unconditional love.

What does it look like to forgive unconditionally? It means that the wrongs you've done to others are not held over your head. It means, there is no secret hatred and no public acts of anger. Unconditional forgiveness erases your own hate and disarms your offender, for you have truly lived on the side of right. It's hard to do. I have not lived your life, or experienced the hurt you may feel from the evil others have done to you, so you must search yourself and consider this unconditional forgiveness. I believe that forgiveness was one of Jesus' greatest messages, one that he was very firm about. I think it is rightly in line with the concept that forgiveness stops the cycle of Karma. In a world of forgiveness, there is no build up of hatred, no starting of wars, no violent counter attacks.

When unconditional love and unconditional forgiveness walk hand in hand, people talk out misunderstandings and listen when the other person speaks. Our ego has taken over ourselves and taught us that we are the most important things and that everyone else takes a back seat to us. When we unconditionally love, we unconditionally listen and understand the root of the problem before conflict can rear its ugly head.

What does it look like when we seek the truth wherever it may be found? It makes each and everyone of us explorers in this massive world. Every turned page of a book is a discovery that brings us one thought closer to enlightenment. Every life you are exposed to has a special lesson for you if you are willing to see it. Every subject under the sun is yours to study and you are not encumbered by religious biases. You can find understanding on things that have always mystified you and spurred your curiosity.

It is rightly said that knowledge is power; and because of this, it is so important to keep learning and seeking the truth wherever it may be found. The truth will lighten your heavy heart and take away the fear that a lack of understanding once kept you in. Why must it be sought after? Because unfortunately, we live in a world that is full of people who want to take your money, your possessions, your emotions, anything they can. The truth keeps you sharp and less gullible to the plans and schemes of those still caught in the web of destruction.

I sincerely hope that what I've shared has

brought you to a new place of introspection. I truly want to live a long and happy life in which I exemplify the good things I have spoken about; it is my daily goal to do so. I want nothing but these good things for you as well. We live in such a fantastic time in which information is so freely available to us. This is a luxury that not everyone in the world has access to. We should take advantage of this gift and spread the news of great discoveries and truths we have found. Remember that world we imagine in which we live in unconditional love and forgiveness with an unrelenting thirst for real truth as our guide. Take it with you and be born again to rebirth.

Gabriel D. Roberts was born in Tacoma, Wa in the late 70's. His continued research in the fields of Science, Spirituality and Anthropology continue to yield more and more exciting discoveries. Not being afraid to challenge his own cosmologies in light of new information, Gabriel D. Roberts continues to put together the puzzle pieces of life in a continued effort to bring enlightenment to himself and to his readers.

Please consider reading RIDING THE FINE

LINE by Gabriel D. Roberts, available at fine book outlets. It follows as a natural progression of thought from BORN AGAIN TO REBIRTH and gives some poignant insights for our lives in the period of history fraught with tumult and uncertainty. For more, visit <u>gabrieldroberts.com</u>.

Made in the USA
San Bernardino, CA
31 August 2014